# FREEDOM OF INFORMATION GUIDE

**WANT Publishing Company**
**1511 K Street, N.W.**
**Washington, DC 20005**

Printed by Catterton Printing Co.,
Washington, D.C.
United States of America

ISBN: 0-942008-03-0

Library of Congress Catalog Card Number: 81-70749

# FREEDOM OF INFORMATION GUIDE

## Table of Contents

# FREEDOM OF INFORMATION GUIDE

## INTRODUCTION

The Federal Government is a vast storehouse of information. While some of this information is routinely made available on request, a good portion of it — often the most useful portion — is not.

Fortunately, a citizen's right of access to Federal Government information has been significantly aided in recent years by the passage of two important pieces of legislation: the Freedom of Information Act and the Privacy Act. These acts guarantee a citizen's right to inspect Government documents, subject only to specific exceptions. That is, unlike prior law on the subject, one is *presumed* under the new legislation to have the right of access to documents he requests, and to have it promptly. If the Government decides otherwise, it must explain its reasons, and this explanation can be challenged in a court of law.

### Wide Range of Documents

The Government generates a wide-range of documents that may, at one point or another, be of public interest. The federal regulatory agencies, for instance, maintain data files on businesses and individuals, including investigation reports, consumer complaints, and product tests on a wide selection of goods and services. Specific examples of non-public information (i.e., information not on public file and not routinely available) that may be released under the Freedom of Information Act (FOIA) includes: corporate product development and marketing practices; background reports on consumer products; data on the efficacy of drugs; the nutritional content of processed foods; safety records of automobiles and airlines; policy statements and interpretations not published in the Federal Register; and so forth. A special section has been included in FREEDOM OF INFORMATION GUIDE (beginning on page 43) that provides, in comprehensive fashion, specific examples of the various kinds of requests being received by major regulatory agencies and the agencies' response to these requests.

### Easy-to-Use Guide

FREEDOM OF INFORMATION GUIDE is intended as an easy-to-use guide to requesting information from the Government under the Freedom of Information and Privacy Acts. A number of states, it should be noted, have passed similar laws that apply to state government information. At one point or another, all of us — whether as consumers, business executives, journalists, lawyers or otherwise — may have a legitimate need to obtain documents, correspondence files, policy memorandum, or other information from the voluminous record base maintained by the Federal Government. These Acts are strong tools the citizen has on behalf of public disclosure.

In seeking information from the Government, the first step we recommend is a simple phone call or letter to the public information office of the agency from which information is sought. The fact that a requester can, if necessary, resort to the pro-disclosure provisions of the FOIA/Privacy Acts often encourages agencies to release documents informally.

### Directory Information

The section below, entitled "FOIA and Related Directories" includes two highly useful directories. The first includes a comprehensive listing of Freedom of Information/Privacy Act personnel; names, addresses, and telephone numbers are included. The second listing gives the address and telephone number of major federal public information offices. Public information offices, as indicated, often serve as a good starting point in one's quest for Government information.

Most agencies maintain a considerable amount of information as matter of public record, and this material is usually readily available. If, however, you do not get a satisfactory response in dealing with an agency's public information office or an official of that agency, you have the right — under the FOIA and the Privacy Act — to make a formal, written request for the documents you seek. The purpose of this guide is to provide the reader with a simple, step-by-step procedure for doing this.

The focus here will be on how to obtain information from the Government using the FOIA/Privacy Acts. We will, however, give some attention to certain criticisms that have arisen concerning the use of the FOIA and proposals to amend the Act.

### Major Sections of Guide

FREEDOM OF INFORMATION GUIDE is divided into the following major sections (see above for detailed Table of Contents, including appendices):

— Guide to the Use of the Freedom of Information and Privacy Acts (beginning on page 5). This section provides a concise, step-by-step guide to obtaining Government information through the use of the FOIA-Privacy Acts. The difference between the two Acts is explained.

— The Freedom of Information Act: Recent Developments (beginning on page 22). Includes a discussion of complaints concerning the FOIA and attempts in the 97th Congress to amend it.

— FOIA and Related Directories (beginning on page 30). This section consists of two directories: (1) Directory of FOIA/Privacy Act personnel, and (2) listing of federal public information offices.

— Recent FOIA Requests (beginning on page 43). Includes a summary of recent FOIA requests made to selected federal agencies and the agencies' response thereto.

### Importance of Information Access

One additional introductory comment: Our rights and obligations under the

Constitution would cease to have much meaning if the operations of Government were shrouded in secrecy. There is, on the other hand, the natural tendency of Government, or any organization for that matter, to release only selected, carefully screened material and withhold the rest. There are good reasons for this. First, there is the time and expense involved in preparing material for public access. Secondly, in the case of Government, there are categories of information that should not be released, for such reasons as national defense or public policy. An example of the latter might be, say, commercial or trade secret material voluntarily submitted by private industry to regulatory agencies, but if freely released to the public difficult to obtain in the future.

So when it comes down to a balancing act — the public's right to know versus the obligation of Government to maintain confidentiality. That is why the FOIA/Privacy Acts are so important in our modern, complex society. They clearly state that the public does indeed have a "right to know" and failure to disclose must be specifically justified.

# FREEDOM OF INFORMATION/PRIVACY ACTS

## Background

In order to assist the public in obtaining information from the Government, the Congress in 1966 passed the Freedom of Information Act. Amendments were later added that encouraged even more disclosure.

The Freedom of Information Act (FOIA) is based on the presumption that government and the information of government belong to the public. The FOIA states that a person has a right of access to any document, file or other record in the possession of any executive agency of the Federal Government — subject to nine specific exemptions. Government employees face the possibility of sanctions if they arbitrarily or capriciously withhold requested information.

Today, more than 16 years after its enactment, the FOIA is being used by extremely diverse groups as a means of obtaining both information generated by the Government and private business data collected by the federal agencies. The Act has been used by competitors, analysts, investors, disgruntled employees, potential and existing adverse litigants, public interest groups, foreign businesses and governments, among many others. Much of the current use of the FOIA is not as originally intended, but it is a fact of the FOIA in operation. (See below section entitled "FOIA — Recent Developments," beginning on page 22.)

Prior to the enactment of the FOIA, the burden was on the individual to prove his right to look at non-public government records. Moreover, there were no clearly delineated statutory guidelines to assist the individual seeking information and no judicial remedies for those wrongfully denied access. With the passage of the FOIA, however, the burden of proof was shifted from the individual to the Government: the "need to know" standard was replaced by the "right to know" doctrine and the burden was placed on Government to justify failure to disclose rather than on the individual to justify right to access.

Further, in 1974 the Privacy Act was enacted. This marked the first time that Congress gave comprehensive statutory recognition to an individual's right of privacy in regard to Government files concerning him. Both the FOIA and the Privacy Act provide for access to Government records. But while the FOIA is designed to be used by individuals seeking many kinds of information, the Privacy Act is intended to assist individuals in obtaining information about themselves and preventing certain disclosure of this information.

More specifically, the Privacy Act allows an individual to review almost all federal files pertaining to himself. It requires that these files be accurate, relevant, and up-to-date, and allows the subjects of the files to challenge the accuracy of the information contained in them. It prescribes that information gathered for one purpose may not be used for another, and that whenever possible, the information be obtained directly from the individual. And perhaps most important of all, it gives the individual significant control over how information concerning him is used. With certain exceptions, it specifies that records containing such personal information be disclosed to others only with the consent of the individual to whom the record pertains. As with the FOIA, civil remedies are available if an agency refuses access or declines to amend or correct a file.

The Privacy Act places restrictions on the disclosure of personally identifiable information and also prescribes that there be no secret record systems on individuals. As with the FOIA, the Privacy Act compels the Government, subject to specific exemptions, to reveal its information sources.

## Which Act To Use

The essential difference between the two Acts is as follows: the Privacy Act requires the disclosure of records containing personal information to the individual who is the subject of the record but restricts such disclosure to others, whereas the FOIA requires that all types of information be released to anyone making a request provided that, among other things, it does not violate an individual's right of privacy. (See discussion of exemptions to the FOIA below, beginning on page 9.)

If you are interested in obtaining documents concerning the general activities of Government, you should make your request under the Freedom of Information Act. If, on the other hand, you are seeking access to Government records pertaining solely to you, you should make your request under the Privacy Act.

Congress intended that the two Acts be considered together in the processing of requests for information. Many Government agencies handle requests under both Acts out of the same office.

Nevertheless, it is still a good idea to make your request in a way that guarantees the fullest possible disclosure. So, if you are uncertain as to which of the Acts will afford the best results, you would be wise to make your request under both the FOIA and the Privacy Act.

## How To Request Documents Under Freedom of Information Act*

The Freedom of Information Act (FOIA) applies only to documents held by administrative agencies of the executive branch of the Federal Government. It does not apply to the deliberations of the inner White House nor to information maintained by the legislative or judicial branches. The executive branch includes most executive departments and offices, military departments, government corporations, government controlled corporations, and independent regulatory agencies. All records in possession of these entities must be released upon request unless one or more of the nine exemptions are applicable.

The FOIA does not obligate federal agencies to do research on your behalf. You cannot, for example, expect the agency to analyze documents or to collect

---

*This section and several that follow are based, in part, on information provided by Freedom of Information Clearinghouse, Washington, D.C.

information it does not have. If, however, the information is on record — a document, a tape recording, a computer printout — the Act can help you obtain access to it.

The only information that may be withheld under the Act is that which falls within any of the nine designated categories. These exemptions from disclosure are discussed below.

## Making The Request

The first step is to determine what you want and state your request as precisely as possible, since the law says your request must "reasonably describe" the records you seek. You do not need to specify a document by name or title. What is necessary is that you provide a description reasonable enough to allow a Government employee who is familiar with the agency's files to locate the records you seek.

If, for example, you want information on nursing homes in your area, it is enough to state that the Government requires annual surveys to be conducted on the nursing home industry, and that you want to see the surveys. Or if you want information on an annual report filed by a corporation, specify the type of report and the agency that requires it. The SEC, for example, has annual, quarterly, and periodic reporting requirements. A number of examples are given below in the section entitled "Recent FOIA Requests."

Your request need only state that it is being made pursuant to the Freedom of Information Act (5 U.S.C. Sec. 552). It may help to write "Freedom of Information Request" (or Appeal) on the envelope and on the top of the letter. With one exception (as noted later), you do not have to explain the reasons for your demands, and Government employees do not have any right to ask. By statute, the only ground an agency has for refusing your demand is proof that the documents do not exist or are specifically covered by one or more of the nine exemptions. The requester does *not* have to prove that he tried to obtain the documents elsewhere and found them unavailable.

An appeal within an agency or department may be necessary if an initial denial is received. An appeal letter should be addressed to the head of the agency and should detail the request and the denial, and state that an appeal is being made of the agency's initial denial. This may involve only a two-or three-sentence letter. Sample FOIA request and appeal letters are given below.

The Government has 10 working days to respond to an initial request and 20 working days to reply to an appeal. These deadlines, in practice, are seldom met by most agencies.

The more precise you make your request, the more prompt your response is likely to be. An agency can delay responding to the substance of your request while seeking "clarification" on what it is you are after. A request, however, that asks for "other related documents" is sometimes appropriate, because agencies seldom volunteer knowledge of other potentially valuable information on the same subject that they may possess.

An agency may respond more quickly if you follow up on a written request with a phone call. If a Government office is aware that you know your rights, it will sometimes move with more dispatch.

Another barrier to information access is cost. The law permits agencies to charge for the direct costs of searching for and copying documents. Agencies cannot lawfully charge for indirect costs, such as the time they spend in determining which portions of documents must be disclosed and which portions may be withheld under the nine exemptions.

To save money on reproduction expenses, you may want to ask to see the documents themselves instead of having copies sent. If you do ask for copies, it may help if you state in your letter that you will pay any costs up to a stated amount but would like to be promptly advised of costs in excess of that amount. If you believe that disclosure of the records you seek will primarily benefit the general public, you should request the agency to waive or reduce its fees. Some agencies, it should be noted, do not charge for copies below a certain amount, such as 50 or 100 copies.

Following on the next page is a sample request letter (See Appendix "C" for additional samples).

## Sample Request Letter

Freedom of Information Unit
(Name and Address of Government Agency)

   Re: Freedom of Information Request

Dear Sir or Madam:

    Pursuant to the Freedom of Information Act, 5 U.S.C. 552, I hereby request access to (or a copy of) (describe the document containing the information that you want).

    If any expenses in excess of $_____ are incurred in connection with this request, please inform me of all such charges prior to their being incurred for my approval.

    Thank you for your prompt attention to this matter.

                Very truly yours,

## Nine Exemptions Under FOIA

Government agencies may refuse to disclose information if it falls within one of nine specified categories. A 1979 U.S. Supreme Court decision, however, held that request for information falling within one or more of the exemptions did not justify the automatic withholding of the information.* Whether or not to disclose was within agency discretion, the Court said.

The Court added, however, that business and financial data may be subject to mandatory withholding under the Trade Secrets Act, 18 USC 1905, a long neglected statute passed by Congress in 1899.

The question as to the withholding of business data has not been resolved and has figured in recent attempts to amend the FOIA. See section below entitled "FOIA-Recent Developments." Also, for publications that discuss legal issues, see section below entitled "Selected FOIA References."

The nine exemptions and the type of information involved under each are as follows:

(b) (1) — (A) specifically authorized under criteria established by an Executive Order to be kept secret in the interest of national defense of foreign policy and (B) are in fact properly classified pursuant to such Executive Order.

The documents exempt under this section are those that are officially stamped Top Secret, Secret, or Confidential, terms which are defined by Presidential Executive Order. Courts, however, will not necessarily take an official's word on the propriety of the classification, and may look at the information itself to see if it is properly classified. This should be especially helpful in securing access to historical records, and documents that were obviously classified merely to prevent domestic political repercussions. Also, the fact that a few pages of a report are properly classified does not mean that the remaining non-sensitive portions can be cloaked in secrecy. Remember, too, that just because information is in the possession of the Departments of Defense or State does not necessarily mean that it is classified. For instance, material such as results of drug-testing done on GIs returning from overseas is not generally classified, and so is not exempt under this provision.

(b) (2) — related solely to the internal personnel rules and practices of an agency.

This exemption covers such things as employee parking and cafeteria regulations, as well as certain manuals that relate only to the internal managment and organization of particular agencies. But staff manuals instructing inspectors or agents on how to perform their jobs are not exempt.

(b) (3) — specifically exempted from disclosure by statute provided that such statute (A) requires that matters be withheld from the public in such a

---

*Chrysler Corp. v. Brown, 441 U.S. 281 (1979).

manner as to leave no discretion on the issue, or (B) establishes particular criteria for withholding or refers to particular types of matters to be withheld.

This exemption covers documents and information specifically exempted from disclosure by other laws. For example, under Section 21(f) of the Federal Trade Commission Improvements Act of 1980, 15 USC 57b-2, which completely revamps the FTC's confidentiality standards, the agency is prohibited from disclosing any material submitted pursuant to compulsory process in a law enforcement proceeding. Prior to the FTC improvements Act, the FTC's practice had been to treat documents subpoenaed during an investigation as "agency records" under Sec. (b)(5) of the FOIA (see below) and thus subject to discretionary disclosure.

Also, Sec. 6(f) of the FTC Improvements Act prohibits disclosure of trade secrets and confidential commercial or financial information which, for the most part, would have been subject to discretionary disclosure under Sec. (b)(4) of the FOIA.

Other examples of when the FOIA (b)(3) section is used to cite exemptions from disclosure under other statutes are income tax returns, patent applications, and completed census forms.

The FOIA (b)(3) exemption provides a means of limiting disclosure under the Act without directly amending the Freedom of Information Act itself. This is what occurred in the FTC Improvements Act. A number of other recently-enacted statutes have done likewise.

(b)(4) — trade secrets and commercial or financial information obtained from a person and privileged or confidential.

The agencies under this section may withhold information only if it is either a trade secret or qualifies as commercial or financial information.

In addition, the Government must prove that the information is confidential and that its disclosure would be likely either to impair the agency's ability to obtain necessary information in the future or to cause substantial competitive injury to the submitter. This exemption applies only to information submitted to the Government; Government-prepared documents are never exempt under this section.

Businesses make extensive use of the FOIA to obtain information on competitors. The same company that submits an FOIA request concerning information the Government may have on a competitor may find that the same competitor has submitted a request on him. This kind of activity was not, for the most part, that intended to be served by the Freedom of Information Act but is a fact of the FOIA in practice. (For discussion of problems associated with the FOIA, see discussion below beginning on page 22.)

Though the focus in this report is on the disclosure of information, let us say a word about the business executive who submits certain information to the Government about his business, either because he is required to do so or does so voluntarily, and is concerned that this information will subsequently be released to a requester under the FOIA. What can the business executive do to protect himself?

It is important that when one submits business data to a federal agency that he be familiar with that agency's policies in regard to the release of trade secret and commercial information. The FOIA (b)(4) exemption, like all FOIA exemptions, is discretionary. That is, even if an agency agrees that business information does qualify under exemption (b)(4), it still has the discretion to disclose it, if it chooses to do so.

Most agencies, however, have procedures through which a company is notified that an FOIA request has come in concerning business data submitted by it and is given an opportunity to make comments to the agency as to whether the data should be withheld under the (b)(4) trade secret exemption. Both the Consumer Product Safety Commission and the Securities & Exchange Commission, for instance, have procedures in this regard. If the agency, after receiving comments, decides that the benefits of disclosure outweigh the company's confidentiality claims, the company, as a last resort, could file a court action to prevent disclosure. The court, of course, may or may not decide in the company's favor.

There has been considerable litigation involving the disclosure of business information. The matter is still quite unsettled in many respects. An excellent discussion of the Freedom of Information Act and recent litigation concerning it is given in the publication, *Federal Information Disclosure* (See "Selected References" below).

As indicated, the statutes under which certain agencies operate serve to increase the protection of information that would otherwise be subject to discretionary disclosure under (b)(4) or one of the other exemptions. The FTC Improvements Act of 1980 has already been mentioned. Another is Sec. 6(b)(1) of the Consumer Product Safety Commission Act, 15 USC 2055(b)(1). This section provides that prior to public disclosure of any information pertaining to a consumer product, the Consumer Product Safety Commission must notify the manufaturer and give it an opportunity to submit comments regarding such information. The Securities & Exchange Commission has recently established regulations regarding trade secret information similar to those in effect at the CPSC.

(b) (5) — inter-agency or intra-agency memoranda or letters which would not be available by law to a party other than an agency in litigation with the agency.

This is the exemption most widely used. In general, two somewhat overlapping dividing lines may be drawn between what must be disclosed and what may be withheld under this exemption. First, factual portions of documents generally should be disclosed, but advice and recommendations on legal and policy matters may be withheld. Second, preliminary drafts, and unfinished reports may be withheld, but once finished, such memoranda and reports should generally be disclosed. To illustrate, a memo from a staff person to a supervisor recommending that a particular policy be established would be exempt except for factual portions. But factual reports or analyses of facts are generally not exempt.

(b) (6) — personnel and medical files and similar files, the disclosure of which would constitute a clearly unwarranted invasion of personal privacy.

This exemption involves a balancing of the public's need to know against the degree of invasion of privacy which would result from disclosure. If your request involves this exemption, a brief explanation of the public benefits from disclosure should be made so that it can be determined whether the invasion of privacy resulting from disclosure would be "clearly unwarranted" as the exemption provides.

(b) (7) — Investigatory records compiled for law enforcement purposes, but only to the extent that the production of such records would (A) interfere with enforcement proceedings, (B) deprive a person of a right to a fair trial or an impartial adjudication, (C) constitute an unwarranted invasion of personal privacy, (D) disclose the identity of a confidential source and, in the case of a record compiled by a criminal law enforcement authority in the course of a criminal investigation, or by an agency conducting a lawful national security intelligence investigation, confidential information furnished only by the confidential source, (E) disclose investigative techniques and procedures, or (F) endanger the life or physical safety of law enforcement personnel.

This is another much used exemption. Under it the Government must prove that the documents were compiled for civil or criminal law enforcement purposes, and that disclosure would actually result in one of the six enumerated harms. Thus, documents such as annual surveys or inspections may be investigatory, but they are, in fact, not compiled for law enforcement purposes and, therefore, not exempt under this section.

(b) (8) — information concerning financial institutions

This section exempts from disclosure matters "contained in or related to examination, operating, or condition reports prepared by, on behalf of, or for the use of, an agency responsible for the regulation or supervision of financial institutions."

This includes, for example, investigatory reports of the Federal Reserve Board concerning federal banks, documents prepared by the Securities Exchange Commission regarding the New York Stock Exchange, and other similar information.

(b) (9) — information concerning wells

Section (b)(9) exempts from disclosure "geological and geophysical information and data, including maps concerning wells."

This provision was added as a specific exemption because at the time of the Act's passage, it was unclear whether this type of information was covered by the trade secret provision of the Act, i.e., exemption (b)(4).

## Appeal Procedure

If your request for information is denied, you should send a letter of appeal to the person or office specified in the agency's reply. If for some reason this information is not provided, file your appeal with the head of the agency. Include a copy of the rejection letter along with a copy of your original request, and make as strong a case as possible for your right of access. It is important to clarify the request if the denial indicates some confusion on the part of the agency as to what is being sought.

If you plan to pursue the matter in court in the event your appeal is denied, you might want to indicate this in your letter.

Most agency regulations require that appeals be made within 30 days after the individual has been notified that his request has been denied. Therefore, if you decide to file an appeal, you should do so within this time frame.

The agency is required to respond to an appeal within 20 working days after receiving it. If, however, the initial request was answered within the 10-day time period, an extension of up to 10 working days may be granted.

If the agency denies your appeal in whole or in part, it must inform you of your right to seek judicial review. If after 20 working days from the time of the agency's receipt of your appeal you have not received a reply, you may take your case to court.

A sample appeal letter follows on the next page:

## Sample Appeal Letter

(Name and Address of Head of Government Agency)

   Re: Freedom of Information Appeal

Dear Secretary _____ :

   By letter dated (month), (day), (year), I requested access to    (use same description as in request letter)   . By letter dated (month), (day), (year), Mr./Mrs. _____ denied my request. Purusant to the Freedom of Information Act, 5 U.S.C. 552, I hereby appeal that denial. I have enclosed a copy of my request letter and the denial that I have received.

   If you do not act upon my appeal within 20 working days I will deem my request denied.

                        Very truly yours,

### Taking FOIA Case to Court

If your appeal is rejected, you may take your case to federal district court. Such action, or course, may involve considerable time and expense.

You can file suit in the U.S. District Court in the district where you live or do business or where the agency records are kept. Or you can take the case to the U.S. District Court in the District of Columbia. Most FOIA litigation does, in fact, occur in that court. See Appendix "D" for an FOIA complaint filed in federal district court.

If you have a strong case, there is a good possibility that your decision to seek judicial review will itself produce results. Unless the agency withholding the information has a well-founded reason for doing so, it may decide to release the material rather than go into litigation.

As a plaintiff under the FOIA, you go into court with the presumption that right is on your side: the burden of proof is on the Government to justify withholding information. Judges are authorized to examine the contents of contested documents to determine whether all or any part of them can be withheld. The law requires that "reasonable segregable portions" of the exempt records be released.

The courts are supposed to expedite FOIA cases and, whenever possible, consider them ahead of other matters. The Act also specifies that court costs and attorney fees be awarded if the plaintiff has "substantially prevailed." In other words, if it is clear that the information should have been released to you in the beginning, the Government may be required to pay the court costs and your attorney's fee. In addition, if the judge finds that agency officials have acted "arbitrarily and capriciously" in withholding information, the Office of Personnel Management (formerly known as the Civil Srvice Comm'n) may initiate proceedings to determine whether disciplinary action is warranted.

Litigation under the FOIA has produced hundreds of U.S. district court and appeals court decisions. If you wish to pursue this further, consult the section below entitled "Selected FOIA References."

### State Laws

The Freedom of Information Act applies only to federal administrative agencies, not to state agencies. Many states, however, have similar statutes. To find out about state laws, look them up in the appropriate state code or write the State Attorney General's office.

### The Sunshine and Advisory Committee Acts

Two important Federal open-meetings laws exist. The Sunshine Act, 5 U.S.C. Sec. 552b, requires multi-headed agencies such as the Civil Aeronautics Board to announce their meetings ahead of time and to open them to the public unless one of nine specific exemptions applies to particular discussions. Similarly, the Federal Advisory Committee Act, 5 U.S.C. App. 1, contains the same requirements regarding meetings of outside groups advising federal agencies.

# THE PRIVACY ACT

In 1974, Congress enacted the Federal Privacy Act, 5 U.S.C. Sec. 552a, which, on the one hand, requires the Government to protect personal information from misuse and unauthorized disclosure and, on the other hand, establishes a right of access for individuals to their own files, and a right to correct those files. The exceptions to an individual's right of access are fewer than those under the Freedom of Information Act. However, law enforcement agencies and the CIA are excepted from the individual access provisions, and there is no specific time limit for an agency's initial response to a request. Thus, requests for your own file would do well to invoke both the Freedom of Information Act and the Privacy Act. (Differences between the FOIA and the Privacy Acts are discussed above, p. 5).

## Information Available Under the Privacy Act

The Privacy Act applies only to personal records maintained by the executive branch of the Federal Government. It does not apply to records held by state and local government or private organizations. The Federal agencies covered by the Act include executive departments and offices, military departments, government corporations, government controlled corporations, and independent regulatory agencies. Subject to specified exceptions, files that are part of a system of records held by these agencies must be made available upon request to the individual subject of the record. A system of records, as defined by the Privacy Act, is a group of records from which information is retrieved by reference to a name or other personal identifier such as a social security number.

The Federal Government is a treasure trove of information concerning individual citizens. For example:

- —If you have worked for a federal agency or government contractor or have been a member of any branch of the armed services, the Federal Government has a file on you.

- —If you have participated in any federally financed project, some agency probably has a record of it.

- —If you have been arrested by local, state, or federal authorities and your fingerprints were taken, the FBI maintains a record of the arrest.

- —If you have applied for a Government subsidy for farming purposes, the Department of Agriculture is likely to have this information.

- —If you have received veterans' benefits, such as mortgage or education loans, employment opportunities, or medical services, the Veterans' Administration has a file on you.

- —If you have applied for or received a student loan or grant certified by the Government, either the Department of Health & Human Services or the Department of Education (these two agencies were formed from the old Department of Health, Education & Welfare) will have recorded this information.

—If you have applied for or been investigated for a security clearance for any reason, there is a good chance that the Department of Defense has a record of it.

—If you have received medicare or social security benefits, the Department of Health & Human Services has a file on you.

In addition, Federal files on individuals include such items as:

—Investigatory reports of the Federal Communications Commission concerning whether individuals holding citizens band and/or amateur radio licenses have violated operating rules.

—Records of the Internal Revenue Service listing the names of individuals entitled to undeliverable refund checks.

—Records compiled by the State Department regarding the conduct of American citizens in foreign countries.

## Disclosure of Records

Agencies are required under the Privacy Act to release records in a form that is "comprehensible." This means that all computer codes and unintelligible notes must be translated into understandable language.

You may examine your records in person or have copies of them mailed to you, whichever you prefer. If you decide that you want to see the records at the agency and for some reason the agency is unable to provide for this, then you cannot be charged copying fees if the records are later mailed to you.

If you view the records in person, you are entitled to take someone along with you. If you do this, you will probably be asked to sign a statement authorizing the agency to disclose and discuss the record in the other person's presence.

Special rules apply to release of medical records. In most cases, when you request to see your medical record, you will be permitted to view it directly. However, if it appears that the information contained in it could have an "adverse effect" on you, the agency may give it to someone of your choice, such as your family doctor, who would be willing to review its contents and discuss them with you.

## Appeal Procedure Under Privacy Act for Denial of Access

A listing of Privacy Act exemptions are given in Appendix B.

Unlike the FOIA, the Privacy Act provides no standard procedure for appealing denials to release information. Many agencies, however, have their own regulations governing this. If your request is denied, the agency should advise you of its appeal procedure and tell you to whom to address your appeal. If this information is not provided, you should send your letter to the head of the agency. Include a copy of the rejection letter along with a copy of your original request and state your reason for wanting access, if you think it will help.

If an agency withholds all or any part of your record, it must tell you which Privacy Act exemption is involved. It should also advise you why it believes the record can be withheld under the Freedom of Information Act since Congress intended that information sought under either the Privacy Act or the FOIA be released unless it could be withheld under both Acts. Therefore, in making your appeal, it would be a good idea to cite both the FOIA and the Privacy Act. Also, it is advisable to explain why you think the exemptions used to deny you access are unjustified.

## Appeal Procedure for Agency Refusal to Amend Records

If an agency refuses to amend your records, it must advise you of the reasons for the refusal as well as the appeal procedures available to you within the agency. It must also tell you to whom to address your appeal. Amendment appeals are usually handled by agency heads or a senior official appointed by the agency head.

Your appeal letter should include a copy of your original request along with a copy of the agency's denial. You should also include any additional information you might have to substantiate your claims regarding the disputed material.

A decision on your appeal must be rendered within 30 working days of the date of its receipt. In unusual circumstances, such as the need to obtain information from retired records or another agency, an additional 30 days may be granted.

If the agency denies your appeal and still refuses to make the changes you request, you have the right to file a brief statement giving your reasons for disputing the record. This statement of disagreement then becomes part of the record and must be forwarded to all past and future recipients of your file. The agency is also permitted to place in your file a short explanation of its refusal to change the record. This, too, becomes a part of your permanent file and is forwarded along with your statement of disagreement.

If your appeal is denied or if the agency fails to act upon it within the specified time, you may take your case to court.

## Taking Privacy Act Case to Court

Under the Privacy Act, you can sue an agency for refusing to release your records, for denial of your appeal to amend a record, and for failure to act on your appeal within a designated time. You can also sue if you are adversely affected by the agency's failure to comply with any of the provisions of the Act. For example, if you are denied a job promotion due to inaccurate, incomplete, outdated, or irrelevant information in your file, you can contest this action in court.

While the Freedom of Information Act requires individuals to use agency appeal procedures before seeking judicial review, the Privacy Act permits individuals to appeal denials of access directly to the courts (although most agencies have their own appeal procedures and you should use them when available). On the other hand, you are required by the Privacy Act to use administrative appeal procedures in contesting agency refusals to amend your records.

Judicial rulings favorable to you could result in the release or amendment of the records in question. In addition, you can obtain money damages if it is proven that you have been adversely affected as a result of the agency's intentional and willful disregard of the Act's provisions. You might also be awarded court costs and attorney fees.

The Act provides criminal penalties for: the knowing and willful disclosure of personal records to those not entitled to receive them, for the knowing and willful failure to publish the existence and characteristics of all record systems, and for the knowing and willful attempt to gain access to an individual's records under false pretenses.

If and when you do decide to go to court, you can file suit in the federal district court where you reside or do business or where the agency records are situated. Or you can take the case to the U.S. District Court in the District of Columbia. Under the Privacy Act, you are required to bring suit within 2 years from the date of the violation you are challenging. However, in cases where the agency has materially or willfully misrepresented information, the statute of limitations runs 2 years from the date you discover the misrepresentation. As with lawsuits brought under the FOIA, the burden is on the agency to justify its refusal to release or amend records.

## Other Rights Provided Under Privacy Act

One of the most important provisions of the Privacy Act is that which requires agencies to obtain an individual's written permission prior to disclosing to other persons or agencies information concerning him, unless such disclosures are specifically authorized under the Act.

Information can be disclosed without an individual's consent under the following circumstances: to employees and officers of the agency maintaining the records who have a need for the information in order to perform their duties; if the information is required to be disclosed under the FOIA; for "routine uses," i.e., uses that are compatible with the purpose for which the information was collected; to the Census Bureau; to the National Archives; to a law enforcement agency upon the written request of the agency head; to individuals acting in behalf of the health or safety of the subject of the record; to Congress; to the General Accounting Office; or pursuant to court order. In all other circumstances, however, the individual who is the subject of the record must give his consent before an agency can divulge information concerning him to others.

Under the Privacy Act, you are also entitled to know to whom information about you has been sent. Agencies must keep an accurate accounting of all disclosures made to other agencies or persons except those required under the FOIA. Moreover, this information must be maintained for at least five years or until the record disclosed is destroyed, whichever is longer. With the exception of disclosures requested by law enforcement agencies, a list of all recipients of information concerning you must be made available upon request. Therefore, if you are interested in knowing who has received records about you, you should write to the Privacy Act officer or the head of the agency and request that an accounting of disclosures be sent to you.

Finally, the Privacy Act places a moratorium upon any new uses of your social security number by federal, state, and local government agencies after January 1, 1975.* No agency may deny you a right, benefit, or privilege to which you are entitled by law because of your refusal to disclose your number unless the disclosure is specifically authorized by statute or regulation.

---

*All federal agencies must publish annually in the *Federal Register* the "routine uses" of the information they maintain.

# SELECTED REFERENCES

1. Legislative history of FOIA: *Freedom of Information Act Source Book*, Act Source Book, Subcomm. on Administrative Practice & Procedure, Comm. on the Judiciary, U.S. Senate, 93rd Cong., 2d Sess. 1974 (S. Doc. No. 93-82).

2. Legislative history of 1974 Amendments: Freedom of Information Act and Amendments of 1974 (P.L. 93-502) Source Book, Subcomm. on Government Information and Individual Rights, Comm. on Government Operations, U.S. House of Representatives, 94th Cong., 1st Sess. 1975.

3. Discussion of business data issues: *Freedom of Information Act Requests for Business Data and Reverse—FOIA Lawsuits*, 25th Report by the Comm. on Government Operations, 95th Cong., 2d Sess. 1978 (H. Rept. No. 95-1382).

4. Compilation and index of cases: U.S. Dept. of Justice *Freedom of Information Case List* (Sept. 1980 ed.).

5. Litigation manual: Center for National Security Studies, *Litigation Under the Federal Freedom of Information Act and Privacy Act* (C. Marwick, ed. — 1980 Edition).

6. General treatise: James O'Reilly, *Federal Information Disclosure* (McGraw Hill 1980).

7. General treatise: *Guidebook to the Freedom of Information and Privacy Acts*. (Clark Boardman Co. 1980).

8. Comprehensive treatment of FOIA: Kenneth Culp Davis, *Administrative Law Treatise* Vo. 1 and supplements (K.C. Davis, Publ. — 2d ed. 1978).

9. Periodic service on information law: *Access Reports* (Washington Monitor, Washington, D.C.) (bi-weekly).

10. Periodic service: *FOIA Update,* published quarterly by the Office of Information Law & Policy, Department of Justice, Room 3127, Washington, D.C. 20532. Available through Superintendent of Documents. GPO, Washingotn, D.C. 20402. Stock No. 027-000-80002-5.

11. Current issues: *News Media & the Law.* Published five times per year by Reporters Committee for Freedom of the Press (Washington, D.C.).

# FREEDOM OF INFORMATION ACT — RECENT DEVELOPMENTS*

The major impetus for freedom of information legislation over the years has come from Congress. The Executive Branch of Government, understandably, has generally been less than enthusiastic about opening its files to public inspection. The problem has been to fashion a compromise, one that offered public accountability concerning Government operations but provided confidentiality when the situation called for it.

In 1946, as part of the Administrative Procedure Act, Congress enacted the first agency-wide open records statute. It promised access to information to persons "properly and directly concerned" with an agency action and permitted the withholding of documents when such was "in the public interest." This broad language, not surprisingly, was used by many agencies to justify withholding information rather than making it available.

Before this legislation had survived its first decade, changes were being recommended; but it was not until 1966 that the Freedom of Information Act was finally passed. The FOIA appeared to be all that advocates of open Government could hope for. Instead of limiting access to those "properly and directly concerned," it told the Government to release information to "any person" unless the information was properly exempt. Instead of giving agencies broad discretion to decide what was and what was not "in the public interest," the FOIA placed the burden squarely on the agencies to justify the withholding of documents. Still Congress was concerned that Govenrment not operate totally in a "fishbowl," nor should it disclose national secrets nor permit law enforcement to be impeded. It crafted nine exemptions to protect these areas and others including: personal privacy, trade secrets, internal agency matters, banking records and gas/oil well data. The FOIA and its nine exemptions were spelled out above. (See discussion beginning on page 9.)

The FOIA was amended in 1974 to meet Congressional objections that it was not being administered by the agencies as intended by the 1966 law. For example, it had become standard practice for an agency to withhold an entire document if even a small part of it contained confidential or secret information. The Amendments required agencies to review documents for exempt information, to segregate the protected portions, and release an edited version of the remaining information. Further it ordered agencies to charge only for the time it took to search for and copy requested documents. Some agencies, according to Congressional testimony, had been charging exorbitant fees. The Amendments, in addition, narrowed somewhat the protections for law enforcement and national security information and set deadlines — 10 business days in most cases — within which agencies were required to respond to FOIA requests.

---

*This section is based on material prepared by Tonda Rush, Reporters Committee for Freedom of the Press (Washington, .D.C.)

## The Forces for Change

The amended law caught Congress by surprise by encouraging a sudden and dramatic upswing in FOIA requests. Requestors soon learned that they could do such things as find out the substance of Government adjudicatory and rulemaking processes that previously had been rather opaque. Businesses learned that they could monitor each others' activities by making FOIA requests of agencies that regulated their industries. Public interest groups began to use the Freedom of Information Act to track environmental law enforcement, affirmative action and consumer safety.

The media began to use the FOIA for story research and — more importantly — as a cudgel to induce agencies to release more information informally. Prisoners turned to their jailhouse lawyers for help in researching the Government's case against them.

It was perhaps inevitable that as the number of requests mounted, so would criticisms as to how the FOIA was being used. The U.S. Justice Department, which oversees how the federal agencies respond to the requirements of FOIA, argues that the Act currently is being used in a number of unintended ways and these unintended uses interfere unduly with certain important governmental activities. The Justice Department also says that the financial burden of complying with the FOIA is dramatically greater than originally anticipated.

## Unintended Uses of FOIA

According to the Justice Department, only a small percentage of FOIA users are those intended as the Act's primary beneficiaries — the news media, scholars, and public interest organizations. In actual practice, the Justice Department says, the vast majority of requests are coming from businesses (and from attorneys on behalf of their business clients) seeking information on their competitors. This use of the FOIA is well illustrated in the section below entitled "Recent FOIA Requests." Further, attorneys are making considerable use of the Act on behalf of litigants in private lawsuits. Such requests, according to Justice, generally seek the fruits of the Government's investigative efforts to buttress private legal claims for damages, not to reveal information to the public. The normal method attorneys use for obtaining information in private litigation is the "discovery" process. Discovery rules require a showing that the requested matter is relevant and can be produced without placing an excessive burden on the respondent. The FOIA, on the other hand, allows litigants to pursue "fishing expeditions" at taxpayers expense, the Justice Department claims.

Examples of other unintended uses, the Justice Department argues, are the numerous requests filed with the Drug Enforcement Administration and the Federal Bureau of Investigation by or on behalf of prisoners seeking information about cohorts in crime or about enforcement methods or sources. FBI Director William Webster has claimed that many of these requests are instigated by inmates seeking to identify the informants who "probably" were responsible for their incarceration.

Further, the Justice Department says that organized crime figures may have used the Act in an effort to identify Government informants. Similarly, the Central Intelligence Agency claims that foreign agents may have used the Act in their search for intelligence information.

## Trade Secret Information

The Government also argues — this time with the business community in its corner — that the pro-disclosure provisions of the FOIA make it difficult for the federal agencies to assure the confidentiality of trade secrets and other sensitive business information submitted by private enterprise. This fact, according to the Justice Department, has made companies increasingly reluctant to submit information to the Government and has diminished the quality of the information that they do provide, both voluntarily and otherwise.

In response to this criticism, a number of agencies have tightened up on their procedures concerning the release of commercial information. But the Justice Department says that regardless of how much actual damage has been done in regard to the release of trade secrets (and some maintain that it has been negligible), there is at least a perception in parts of the business community that commercially valuable information submitted to the Government is vulnerable to disclosure under the FOIA.

In theory, sensitive business information is protected by Exemption (b)(4) of the FOIA, which permits, though does not require, agencies to withhold "trade secrets and commercial or financial information." The business community, however, argues that Exemption (b)(4) has been weakened by a series of court decisions. The most damaging, from the point of view of business, was a holding in 1974 by the U.S. Court of Appeals for the District of Columbia that material considered confidential can be withheld only when it can be shown that disclosure will cause "substantial" competitive harm. And even if major competitive harm can be shown, disclosure is still within agency discretion.

## Oversight Hearings

In 1977, the first formal oversight hearings were held in the Senate since the passage of amendments to the FOIA three years earlier. The Federal Trade Commission testified that businesses were beginning to refuse to turn over information to it without a subpoena because they feared the information would not be properly protected. The Food & Drug Administration testified that editing out trade secrets in responding to FOIA requests was costly and time-consuming. The Environmental Protection Agency and other agencies handling business information echoed similar complaints. The FBI objected that its task of protecting the privacy of persons named in law enforcement records was difficult under the mandates of FOIA. The CIA testified that the amendments to the FOIA in 1974 has been "traumatic" to intelligence officers trained to work under cover. The Act, it said, has chilled sensitive intelligence sources abroad. A number of bills to amend the FOIA were submitted in response to the hearing but they did not get out of committee.

By 1980, the agencies were agitating even more vocally for changes. The CIA asked for total exemption from the FOIA. The FBI sought a "moratorium" on the release of its records for a period fo five to 10 years. Most agencies asked for a different fee schedule to allow them to recover more of the costs of administering the Act. And the battle was joined by business interests looking for more trade secret protection.

## Release of Commercial Information

The momentum to amend the FOIA was helped along by an incident that riled one industry — the tobacco growers. Pursuant to an FOIA request, the FTC released a report on the tobacco industry produced by the Roper Organization for the Tobacco Institute. The document had been intended by Roper for the internal use of the organization and its members but had been provided to the FTC at its request. The FTC then released it in respnse to an FOIA request.

The release of the report, which Roper considered to contain confidential commerical information, enraged the tobacco industry. It added its voice to the clamor for Freedom of Information Act reform.

Senator Wendell Ford of Kentucky heeded the complaint against the FTC. He proposed in the 96th Congress (1979-80) stringent restrictions on the FTC's release of information. The proposal was added to the FTC improvements Act of 1980. Under the Act, the FTC was prohibited from releasing information provided to it by business until such information was introduced formally as evidence in an enforcement proceeding.

A bill to exempt from the FOIA, Commerce Department information about quantity, price, destination and foreign buyers of domestic goods passed in the 96th Congress as well. Bills to exempt the CIA and to institute the FBI's requested moratorium were introduced but never enacted.

Another illustration shows how use of the Freedom of Information Act to obtain commercial information can sometimes pit small business against big business.

A few big companies make ships, planes, tanks, trucks and communications equipment for the military, and they usually get the lucrative contracts for spare parts for their equipment.

To bid against them, a small supplier must have access to technical information about the piece of equipment. Before the FOIA, the military more often then not refused to provide the information. Now, under the Act, such information is subject to public disclosure. Proposals to amend the FOIA, however (see below), would prevent the release of most information of this nature.

## Further Attempts to Amend

The Freedom of Information Act remained largely intact as the 97th Congress (1981-1982) convened in January 1981. This Congress, however, was considerably more conservative than its predecessor and was ready to give a more sympathetic ear to agencies' complaints about the burdens imposed by the Act. A number of bills that would substantially amend the FOIA were introduced. Changes began.

In late 1981, the Justice Department, under Attorney General William French Smith, issued a memorandum tightening up on the release of information by the department. In addition, Congress amended authorization legislation for the Consumer Product Safety Commission to provide greater protection for business-related information held by the commission. Under this legislation, the commission:

(1) May not release "commercial or financial information obtained from a person, nor may it release confidential information or "trade secrets."

(2) May not release other information obtained from businesses in its day-to-day activities until it has notified the business of its intention, provided a summary of the information contemplated for release, taken steps to assure the accuracy of the information and determined that disclosure is reasonably related to the statutory purposes of the agency. After it has taken comments from the company involved, it may not release the information for at least 10 days after notifying the company, once again, that it has decided on release, unless health and safety requirements dictate a shorter period.

(3) May not release information collected during an investigation concerning a ban on hazardous substance until a complaint is issued in the investigation, a remedial settlement agreement has been entered or the submitter agrees to the disclosure.

The major effect of this legislation, as well as that described above involving the Federal Trade Commission, is to limit agency discretion in releasing information that may fall under the (b)(4) — trade secrets, commercial and financial data — exemption to the FOIA.

## Internal Revenue Service Exemption

The Internal Revenue Service became enmeshed in court litigation concerning a Freedom of Information Act request and finally took its case to Congress.

A private economist, active in analysis of Internal Revenue Service procedures and effectiveness, made an FOIA request in 1975 for computerized information from the agency's Taxpayer Compliance Measurement Program. The IRS refused to release it. The analytic information the economist asked for, the IRS said, included taxpayers' names and thus the privacy of these taxpayers would be infringed. A federal district court in Seattle ordered the IRS to remove the names and release the rest of the information. The IRS appealed the ruling and the documents were ordered withheld pending the outcome on appeal.

The economist who had made the FOIA request then discovered that the IRS had already released the expurgated versions of the computer tapes to another

Government agency, the Bureau of Economic Analysis. An FOIA request was then submitted to BEA. BEA denied the request, also pleading taxpayer privacy. A second series of court decisions ensued, all resulting in decisions ordering release of the expurgated tapes. But in a number of legal maneuvers, the Government refused to hand over the material. Finally, the Ninth Circuit Court of Appeals in San Francisco unequivocally ordered the release of the tapes. The Government then obtained an order from the U.S. Supreme Court staying the release of the information pending Supreme Court review of the case.

But rather than risk yet another unfavorable court ruling, the IRS went to Capitol Hill for relief. It succeeded in getting a provision tacked on to the Economic Recovery Tax Act of 1981 regarding FOIA requests for IRS statistics and audit information. The provision stated: "Nothing in. . . any provision of law shall be construed to require the disclosure of standards used. . . for the selection of returns for examination. . ., if the Secretary determines that such disclosure will seriously impair assessment, collection or enforcement under the internal revenue laws." This gives the IRS broad discretion to withhold information if it has a tangential relation to the tax-auditing process.

### Recent Congressional Hearings

During 1981, both Houses of Cognress held hearings on proposals to amend the Freedom of Information Act. In a hearing in October 1981, the Justice Department aired complaints that the FOIA was too expensive, having cost approximately $50 million to administer in 1980. The Justice Department said that the Act's time limits serve to bog down agencies in FOIA matters and prevented more important duties from being done. Also, the department said, informants for the FBI and CIA were afraid their anonymity was not being protected in files covered by the FOIA and businesses were complaining that trade secrets were being released and that the Act had become a tool for industrial piracy.

Groups testifying on behalf of the FOIA countered that the $50 million is well worth the benefits conferred and negligible in relation to most other Government programs. The groups said that the 10-day time limit was in fact not being observed by most agencies and that no one had shown with convincing evidence that CIA/FBI informants' identities had been exposed or that businesses had been damaged by trade secret information being released.

Emerging in large part from these hearings was a proposed bill currently pending in the Senate Judiciary Committee (S.1730). This bill, which the Reagan Administration could be expected to support, would:

1) Increase the cost of using the Act by permitting agencies to charge for review time. Fees would continue to be waived if the information would primarily benefit the general public and not the commercial interest of the requester.

2) Lengthen the time limits for agencies to respond, to permit up to 80 days for many requests.

3) Provide businesses legal standing to sue the Government to block disclosure of sensitive commercial information.

4) Broaden the (b)(4) trade secrets exemption to provide greater protection for business information.

5) Change the law enforcement exemption to protect not only the purely investigatory files but any law enforcement files generally.

6) Permit the Attorney General to seal files relating to terrorism, foreign counterintelligence and organized crime.

7) Permit the Government, for the first time, to hold the equivalent of a copyright for information and to charge a fair market value for certain "commercially valuable technological information."

8) Trim courts' power to order the CIA to disclose information.

9) Permit withholding of information submitted to the U.S. by an outside party during the settlement of a lawsuit in which the U.S. "is a party or has an interest."

The proposals embodied in this bill represent potentially dramatic changes to the Freedom of Information Act. The bill would give Government more reasons to withhold information it chooses to keep secret and less latitude to disclose information it desires to let out. Critics of the proposals argue, for example, that they would absolutely bar the disclosure of the confidential business information contained in the trade secrets exemption to the FOIA unless an overriding public safety concern intervened. Currently, agencies may disclose virtually any information that falls within the (b)(4) exemption, or any of the other exemptions for that matter, if they deem it in the public interest to do so.

Whether Congress would approve major changes to the FOIA of this nature is doubtful. While there appears to be broad sentiment in both the House and Senate that certain "fine-tuning" of the Act may be called for, considerably less enthusiasm is evident for a major overhaul. Still, the forces on both sides of the issue promise to lobby hard for their respective positions and a spirited public debate seems assured.

## Conclusion

It was not until 1966 that citizens won from their Government a muscular statutory right to inspect federal agency documents. This landmark legislation, the Freedom of Information Act, was overhauled in 1974 to further strengthen citizen access.

The current efforts to amend the FOIA focus on limiting access, rather than further expanding it. There appears at this time, however, no broad consensus in Congress that major changes are called for, though there may be general support for certain "fine-tuning" adjustments.

Even if the FOIA itself is not directly amended to limit access, the same effect has already been accomplished indirectly, by legislation that relates to the release of information by specific agencies. Legislation in this regard has been enacted for a number of agencies, including the Consumer Product Safety Commission, the Federal Trade Commission, and the Internal Revenue Service, which were discussed above.

Certain changes in the Freedom of Information Act may be appropriate. Still the Act, as it currently exists, recognizes that, even in a democracy, some secrets are needed for effective government. While the FOIA opens many records to public inspection, it exempts access in nine broad areas of information. As indicated, for example, the Government may refuse to give out records concerning military secrets. It may withhold information on law-enforcement investigations and business trade secrets, among other things. While the Act applies in general to federal agencies, it does not, by design, cover the inner White House. Nor does it apply to the judiciary and the Congress.

Even with these exemptions, the Freedom of Information Act has resulted in an era of openness in Government that has been unmatched in the nation's history.

# FOIA AND RELATED DIRECTORIES

## FREEDOM OF INFORMATION/PRIVACY ACT DIRECTORY

The directory below provides a comprehensive listing of agency Freedom of Information and Privacy Act officers, including names, addresses, and telephone numbers.

Under the FOIA, each agency is responsible for setting up its own implementing regulations. The Justice Department is the coordinating agency in this regard. For general information concerning the FOIA/Privacy Acts, you may want to contact the following Justice Department office: Office of Information Law & Policy, Justice Department, 10th & Constitution Ave. N.W., Washington, D.C. 20530 (202) 633-2674.

If you have a general question on the kinds of information available from a particular agency, we suggest you first contact the agency's Public Information Office (see below, p. 38). For more specific questions relating to the release of generally non-public information, the FOIA/Privacy Act names and numbers listed here will be useful.

### ACTION

Ms. Irma Dunnington (202) 254-8103
Management Analyst
Administration Services Division
ACTION
Washington, DC 20525

Mr. Stewart Davis (202) 254-8850
Associate General Counsel
ACTION
806 Connecticut Ave., N.W.
Washington, DC 20525

### AGENCY FOR INTERNATIONAL DEVELOPMENT

Mr. James W. McCulla (202) 632-8628
Director
Office of Public Affairs
Agency for International Development
Department of State
Washington, DC 20523

Mr. Kenneth E. Fries (202) 632-8218
Assistant General Counsel
Office of Employee and Public Affairs
Agency for International Development
Department of State
Washington, DC 20523

### AGRICULTURE DEPARTMENT

Mr. Hal R. Taylor (202) 447-7903
Office of Government and Public Affairs
U.S. Department of Agriculture
Washington, DC 20250

Mr. Jeff Ross (202) 447-4147
Office of the General Counsel
Room 2337-South Bldg.
Department of Agriculture
Washington, DC 20250

### CENTRAL INTELLIGENCE AGENCY

Mr. Ernest Mayerfield (202) 351-6378
Associate General Counsel
Central Intelligence Agency
Washington, DC 20505

### CIVIL AERONAUTICS BOARD

Ms. Phyllis Kaylor (202) 673-5436
FOIA Officer
Civil Aeronautics Board
1825 Connecticut Ave., N.W.
Washington, DC 20428

Ms. Carol Light (202) 673-5791
Attorney/Advisor
Office of the General Counsel
Civil Aeronautics Board
1825 Connecticut Ave., N.W.
Washington, DC 20428

### COMMERCE DEPARTMENT

Ms. Marilyn Mclennan (202) 377-4217
Information Management Division
Office of Organization and
    Management Systems
Department of Commerce
Washington, DC 20230

Mr. Joseph M. Levine (202) 377-5384
Attorney/Advisor
Office of the General Counsel
Room 5879
Department of Commerce
Washington, DC 20230

## COMMISSION ON CIVIL RIGHTS

Mr. Lawrence B. Glick (202) 254-3070
Solicitor
U.S. Commission on Civil Rights
Room 710
1121 Vermont Ave., N.W.
Washington, DC 20425

## COMMODITY FUTURES TRADING COMMISSION

Ms. Lynn Gilbert (202) 254-3382
Deputy Director
Office of Public Information
Commodity Futures Trading Commission
2033 K St., N.W.
Washington, DC 20581

Mr. Wliiam E. Gressman (202) 254-5529
Special Counsel
Office of the General Counsel
Commodity Futures Trading Commission
2033 K St., N.W.
Washington, DC 20581

## COMMUNITY SERVICES ADMINISTRATION

Mr. Roger Schwartz (202) 653-7520
Community Services Administration
Office of the General Counsel
1200 19th St., N.W., Rm. 527
Washington, DC 20506

## CONSUMER PRODUCT SAFETY COMMISSION

Mr. Todd Stevenson (301) 492-6800
FOIA Officer
1111 18th St., N.W.
Washington, DC 20207

Mr. Alan Schoem (202) 634-7770
Asst. General Counsel
U.S. Consumer Product Safety Commission
Washington, DC 20207

## COUNCIL ON ENVIRONMENTAL QUALITY

Mr. Ernest Miner (202) 395-4506
Council on Environmental Quality
722 Jackson Place, N.W.
Washington, DC 20006

## DEFENSE DEPARTMENT

**Legal**

Mr. Robert Gilliat (202) 697-9341
Assistant General Counsel (MHPA) FOIA
DOD/Office of Secretary of Defense
Room 3E999
The Pentagon
Washington, DC 20301

Major James M. Messer (202) 694-2510
Judge Advocate Division (Code JAR)
HQMC, Room 1003
Washington, DC 20380

Lt. Commander White (202) 325-9870
Office of the Judge Advocate General
Department of the Navy
200 Stovall Street
Alexandria, VA 22332

Mr. Theodore T. Belazis (202) 692-7186
Office of the General Counsel
Department of the Navy
Crystal Plaza, Building 5, Room 480
Arlington, VA 20360

Mr. Timothy Hatch (202) 695-3306
Assistant to the General Counsel
Office of the General Counsel
Department of the Army
Washington, DC 20310

Major Alan C. Ernst (202) 694-4075
HQ USAF/JACM
Washington, DC 20330

Major Jay Rowland (202) 693-5740
HQ USAF/JACL
1900 Half Street, S.W.
Washington, DC 20324

Mr. John Wren (202) 695-6552
Assistant General Counsel for Personal &
   Fiscal Matters
Office of the General Counsel (SAF/GC)
Department of the Air Force
The Pentagon, Room 4C941
Washhington, D.C. 20330

**Administrative**

Mr. Charles W. Hinkle (202) 697-4325
Director, Freedom of Information
Department of Defense
OASD (PA); 2C757
The Pentagon
Washington, DC 20301

Major H. W. Gardner (202) 694-3408
Head, Plans and Policy Branch
Division of Public Affairs
U.S. Marine Corps
HQMC (Code PAP) Room 1132
Washington, DC 20380

Mr. Donald Carr (202) 697-1459
Freedom of Information Coordinator
Office of the Chief
Naval Records Management Division
Department of the Navy
OP-09B1; Room 4D71
The Pentagon
Washington, DC 20350

Mr. Guy Oldakei (202) 693-7830
Records Management Division
Office of the Adjutant General
Department of the Army
Attn: DAAG-AMR-S
Room GA080, Forrestal Building
Washington, DC 20314

Ms. Sybil L. Taylor (202) 697-1180
FOIA Specialist (Branch Chief)
Office of the Assistant Secretary of
    Defense (Public Affairs)
Freedom of Information & Security Review
Room 2C757
The Pentagon
Washington, DC 20301

Ms. Anne Wilkinson (202) 697-3467
Freedom of Information Officer
Department of the Air Force
HQUSAF/DAA (S); Room 4A1088H
The Pentagon
Washington, DC 20330

## DEFENSE INTELLIGENCE AGENCY

Ms. Penny Underall (202) 692-5766
Office of the Director
RTS-2A
Washington, DC 20301

## DEFENSE LOGISTICS AGENCY

Mr. Thomas Fereday (202) 274-6047
Records Management Branch
DLA-XA
Cameron Station
Alexandria, VA 22314

## EDUCATION DEPARTMENT

Mr. Jack Billing (202) 426-6573
Office of Public Affairs
Department of Education
FOB-6, Rm. 4169
400 Maryland Ave., S.W.
Washington, DC 20201

Mr. William Werksman (202) 755-1106
General Counsel
Room 4091, FOB 6
400 Maryland Ave., S.W.
Washington, DC 20202

## ENERGY DEPARTMENT

Mr. Milton Jordan (202) 252-5955
Director, Division of FOI/PA Activities
Room 5B138, Forrestal Bldg.
Washington, DC 20585

Mr. Kenneth Cohen (202) 252-8665
Assistant General Counsel for Legal Counsel
1000 Independence Avenue
Forrestal Building
Washington, DC 20004

## ENVIRONMENTAL PROTECTION
## AGENCY

Ms. Jeralene B. Green (202) 755-2674
FOI Specialist
FOI Office (A-101)
U.S. Environmental Protection Agency
401 M Street, S.W.
Washington, DC 20406

Mr. Charles Breece (202) 426-9450
Office of the General Counsel
Grants, Contracts and General
    Administration Division (A-134)
U.S. Environmental Protection Agency
401 M Street, S.W.
Washington, DC 20406

## EQUAL EMPLOYMENT OPPORTUNITY
## COMMISSION

Mr. Anthony De Marco (202) 634-6595
Associate General Counsel
Legal Counsel Division
Equal Employment Opportunity Commission
Room 2254
Washington, DC 20506

## EXECUTIVE OFFICE OF THE PRESIDENT

Ms. Linda L. Smith (202) 395-7097
FOIA Officer
Office of Management and Budget
Executive Office of the President
Washington, DC 20503

## EXPORT-IMPORT BANK

Mr. Stephen G. Glazer (202) 566-8864
Export-Import Bank of the U.S.
811 Vermont Ave., N.W.
Washington, DC 20571

## FARM CREDIT ADMINISTRATION

Mr. Ronald H. Erickson (202) 755-2170
FOIA Officer
490 L'Enfant Plaza, S.W.
Washington, DC 20578

Mr. Robert McLean (202) 755-2143
Assistant General Counsel
Farm Credit Administration
490 L'Enfant Plaza East, S.W.
Washington, DC 20578

## FEDERAL AVIATION ADMINISTRATION

Ms. Susan Holloway (202) 426-3485
Freedom of Information Program Officer
Federal Aviation Administration
400 Seventh St., S.W.
Washington, DC 20590

## FEDERAL COMMUNICATIONS COMMISSION

Mr. Norman Blumenthal (202) 632-6690
Office of the General Counsel
Federal Communications Commission
1919 M St., N.W.
Washington, DC 20554

## FEDERAL DEPOSIT INSURANCE CORPORATION

Ms. Mary E. Anton (202) 389-4261
Bank Regulation Section, Legal Division
Federal Deposit Insurance Corporation
550 17th St., N.W., Rm. 4105A
Washington, DC 20552

## FEDERAL ELECTION COMMISSION

Mr. Fred S. Eiland (202) 523-4065
FOI Officer
Federal Election Commission
1325 K St., N.W.
Washington, DC 20463

Mr. Vincent Convery (202) 523-4000
Attorney
Federal Election Commission
1325 K St., N.W.
Washington, DC 20463

## FEDERAL ENERGY REGULATORY COMMISSION

Mr. John Morrison (202) 357-8049
FOIA Officer
Federal Energy Regulatory Commission
Washington, DC 20426

## FEDERAL HOME LOAN BANK BOARD

Mr. William L. VanLenten (202) 377-6463
Attorney
Federal Home Loan Bank Board
1700 G St., N.W.
Washington, DC 20552

## FEDERAL LABOR RELATIONS AUTHORITY

Mr. Robert J. Freehling (202) 254-9592
Solicitor
Federal Labor Relations Authority
1900 E St., N.W.
Washington, DC 20424

## FEDERAL MARITIME COMMISSION

Mr. Francis C. Hurney (202) 523-5725
Secretary
Federal Maritime Commission
Washington, DC 20573

## FEDERAL MEDIATION & CONCILIATION SERVICE

Ms. nancy Brobb (202) 653-5305
Associate General Counsel
Federal Mediation and Conciliation Service
2100 K St., N.W.
Washington, DC 20427

## FEDERAL MINE SAFETY & HEALTH REVIEW COMMISSION

Ms. Penny Stetina (202) 653-5610
General Counsel
Room 630
1730 K St., N.W.
Washington, DC 20006

## FEDERAL RESERVE BOARD

Mr. William W. Wiles (202) 452-3684
Secretary, Board of Governors
Federal Reserve Board
Washington, DC 20551

Mr. Stephen L. Siciliano (202) 452-3290
Senior Attorney, Legal Division
Federal Reserve Board
Washington, DC 20551

## FEDERAL TRADE COMMISSION

Mr. Keith Golden (202) 532-3582
Office of Freedom of Information
Federal Trade Commission
Sixth and Pennsylvania Ave., N.W.
Washington, DC 20580

Ms. Alexandra P. Buek (202) 523-3855
Assistant to General Counsel
Federal Trade Commission
Sixth and Pennsylvania Ave., N.W.
Washington, DC 20580

## FOOD & DRUG ADMINISTRATION

Department of Health & Human Services
(301) 443-6310
Food & Drug Administration
Freedom of Information-HFI-35
Rm. 12A16
5600 Fishers Lane
Rockville, MD 20851

## GENERAL SERVICES ADMINISTRATION

Ms. Rebecca Thompson (202) 566-1460
Attorney/Advisor, Information & Privacy
General Services Administration
18th and F Sts., N.W.
Washington, DC 20405

## HEALTH & HUMAN SERVICES

Mr. Russ Roberts (202) 472-7453
Departmental FOIA Office
HEW/OPA
HHH Room 118F
Department of Health & Human Services
200 Indiana Ave., S.W.
Washington, DC 20201

Ms. Mary Goggin, Chief (202) 245-7743
Administrative Law Branch
Office of the General Counsel, Rm. 5362
North Bldg.
Department of Health & Human Services
330 Independence Ave., S.W.
Washington, DC 20201

## HOUSING AND URBAN DEVELOPMENT

Ms. Velma Chandler (202) 755-6420
FOIA Officer
HUD Building, Rm. 1104
451 7th St., S.W.
Washington, DC 20410

Ms. Joan Saleschin (202) 755-7087
Attorney/Advisor
HUD Building, Rm. 10252
451 7th St., S.W.
Washington, DC 20410

## INTERIOR DEPARTMENT

Mr. John D. Trezise (202) 343-5216
Division of General Law
Office of the Solicitor
Department of Interior
Washington, DC 20240

## INTERNAL REVENUE SERVICE

Mr. A. James Golato (202) 566-4743
Assistant to Commissioner
Internal Revenue Service
1111 Constitution Ave., N.W.
Washington, DC 20224

## INTERNATIONAL COMMUNICATION AGENCY

Mr. John A. Lindburg (202) 724-9247
Assistant General Counsel
International Communication Agency
1750 Pennsylvania Ave., N.W.
Washington, DC 20547

## INTERSTATE COMMERCE COMMISSION

Mr. Arnold Smith (202) 75-7076
FOIA/Privacy Act Officer
Room 3387, ICC Building
Washington, DC 20423

## DEPARTMENT OF JUSTICE

### FOIA Coordinator

Mr. William J. Snider (202) 633-3452
Administrative Counsel
Justice Management Division
Room 6241, Main Justice
Washington, DC 20530

### Antitrust Division

Mr. Leo Neshkes (202) 633-2692
Chief, Legal Procedure Unit
Room 7416 Main, Antitrust Division
10th and Constitution Ave., N.W.
Washington, DC 20530

### Board of Immigration Appeals

Mr. John Hodgdon (202) 724-6840
Staff Attorney
Room 1122, Main Justice

### Civil Division

Ms. Carolyn Brammer (202) 633-3062
Special Assistant
Room 3616 Main

### Civil Rights Division

Ms. Salliann M. Dougherty (202) 633-3925
FOI/PA Officer
Room 7613 Main

### Community Relations Service

Ms. Polly Kinnibrugh (202) 724-7377
Staff Attorney
Room 642 TODD

**Criminal Division**

Mr. E. Ross Buckley (202) 724-6995
Attorney in Charge
Room 312 FTRI

**Deputy Attorney General**

Ms. Linda Robinson (202) 633-4082
Paralegal Specialist
Room 4314 Main

**Drug Enforcement Administration**

Domenick Mingione (202) 633-5236
Senior Attorney
Room 200 EYE

**Executive Office for U.S. Attorneys**

Mr. Les Rowe (202) 633-4024
Attorney/Advisor
Room 4121 Main

**Federal Bureau of Investigation**

Mr. Dennis Miller (202) 324-3756
Unit Chief
Room 6280, JEH

**Immigration and Naturalization Service**

Ms. Marye D. Gannett (202) 633-3278
FOIA/PA Reviewing Officer
Room 5122 CAB

**Improvements in the Administration of Justice**

Mr. Peter F. Rient (202) 633-4603
Senior Counsel in OIAJ
Room 4238 Main

**Land and Natural Resources Division**

Mr. Vance Hughes (202) 633-2586
Legislative Assistant
Room 2611 Main

**Law Enforcement Assistance Administration**

Mr. William Joyce (202) 376-3696
Attorney/Advisor
Room 1268 IND

**Legal Counsel**

Ms. Mary Lawton (202) 633-2059
Deputy Assistant Attorney General
Room 5224 Main

**Legislative Affairs**

Robin Skinner (202) 633-4054
Legislative Advisor
Room 1133 Main

**Professional Responsibility**

Mr. Jerry Davis (202) 633-2236
Assistant Counsel
Room 4313 Main

**Public Information**

Mr. Mark Sheehan (202) 633-2014
Assistant Director
Room 5114 Main

**Solicitor General**

Mr. Frank Easterbrook (202) 633-2208
Deputy Solicitor General
Room 5609 Main

**Tax Division**

Mr. Donald J. Gavin (202) 724-6430
Assistant Section Chief
Room 3121 STAR

**U.S. Marshals Service**

Mr. Lawrence E. Fischer (202) 285-1121
FOI/PA Officer
Room 205 TCC
Tysons Corner Center
McLean, VA 22102

**U.S. Parole Commission**

Mr. Herman Levy (202) 724-3116
Control Officer
Room 846 HOLC

Mr. William J. Snider (202) 633-4165
Administrative Counsel
Office of Management and Finance
Room 1118 Main

Mr. Quinlan J. Shea (202) 633-4082
Director
Office of Privacy and Information Appeals
Room 4310 Main

**Pardon Attorney**

Mr. Raymond Theim (202) 724-6302
Attorney/Advisor
Room 807 HOLC

## LABOR DEPARTMENT

Ms. Sofia P. Petters (202) 523-6807
Counsel for Administrative Legal Services
Office of the Solicitor
Department of Labor
Room N2428
200 Constitution Ave., N.W.
Washington, DC 20210

## LIBRARY OF CONGRESS

Dr. Harold C. Relyea (202) 287-5821
Specialist
American National Government
Congressional Research Service
The Library of Congress
Washington, DC 20540

Ms. Dorothy Schrader (202) 557-8731
General Counsel
Copyright Office
Washington, DC 20559

## NATIONAL AERONAUTICS & SPACE ADMINISTRATION

Ms. Helen S. Kupperman (202) 755-3927
Assistant General Counsel
Headquarters - NASA
Washington, DC 20545

## NATIONAL LABOR RELATIONS BOARD

Mr. Standau Weinbrecht (202) 254-9275
Acting Associate General Counsel
Division of Enforcement Litigation
National Labor Relations Board
Room 1070
Washington, DC 20570

## NATIONAL MEDIATION BOARD

Mr. Ronald M. Etters (202) 523-5944
General Counsel
National Mediation Board
1425 K St., N.W.
Washington, DC 20572

## NATIONAL SCIENCE FOUNDATION

Mr. Arthur Kusinski (202) 357-9445
Assistant to the General Counsel
National Science Foundation
Washington, DC 20550

## NATIONAL SECURITY COUNCIL

Mr. Robert Kimmit (202) 395-4970
Staff Counsel
National Security Council
Executive Office Building
Washington, DC 20506

## NATIONAL TRANSPORTATION SAFETY BOARD

Mr. John M. Stuhldreher (202) 472-6033
General Counsel
National Transportation Safety Board
Washington, DC 20594

## NUCLEAR REGULATORY COMMISSION

Mr. John Carr (202) 492-8133
Chief, FOI and Privacy Branch
Office of Administration
U.S. Nuclear Regulatory Commission
Washington, DC 20555

Mr. Edward C. Shomaker (202) 492-7242
Office of Executive Legal Director
U.S. Nuclear Regulatory Commission
Washington, DC 20555

## OCCUPATIONAL SAFETY & HEALTH REVIEW COMMISSION

Mr. Earl Ohman (202) 634-4015
Acting General Counsel
Occupational Safety and Health Review
　Commission
1825 K St., N.W.
Washington, DC 20006

## OFFICE OF MANAGEMENT AND BUDGET

Ms. Linda L. Smith (202) 395-4790
Assistant to Director for Administration
Washington, DC 20503

William N. Nichols (202) 395-4550
General Counsel
Executive Office of the President
Washington, DC 20503

## OFFICE OF PERSONNEL MANAGEMENT

Mr. Stuart Rick (202) 632-4600
Information and Privacy Counsel
Office of the General Counsel
Office of Personnel Management
Washington, DC 20415

## OFFICE OF SCIENCE & TECHNOLOGY

Mr. William Montgomery (202) 395-4692
Executive Officer
Office of Science and Technology
Room 3025
Executive Office Building
Washington, DC 20500

## OVERSEAS PRIVATE INVESTMENT CORPORATION

Mr. Ralph T. Mabry (202) 632-1766
Assistant General Counsel for Claims
1129 20th St., N.W.
Overseas Private Investment Corporation
Washington, DC 20527

## PENSION BENEFIT GUARANTY CORPORATION

Mr. William Fitzgerald (202) 254-4827
Disclosure Officer
Office of the Executive Director
2020 K Street, N.W.
Washington, DC 20006

Ms. Nina Hawes (202) 254-3010
Office of the General Counsel
Pension Benefit Guaranty Corporation
2020 K St., N.W.
Washington, DC 20006

## POSTMASTER GENERAL

Mr. Charles D. Hawley (202) 245-4584
Assistant General Counsel
Legal Affairs Division
The Postmaster General
United States Postal Service
Washington, DC 20260

## SECURITIES & EXCHANGE COMMISSION

Mr. Edward A. Wilson (202) 523-5530
FOIA/Privacy Officer
Securities & Exchange Commission
Washington, DC 20549

Mr. John P. Sweeney (202) 272-2454
Assistant General Counsel
Office of the General Counsel
Securities & Exchange Commission
Washington, DC 20549

## SELECTIVE SERVICE SYSTEM

Mr. Clarence E. Boston (202) 724-0419
Records Manager
Selective Service System
Washington, DC 20435

Mr. Henry N. Williams (202) 724-0895
General Counsel
Selective Service System
600 E St., N.W.
Washington, DC 20435

## SMALL BUSINESS ADMINISTRATION

Mr. Nicholas Kalcounos (202) 653-6460
FOIA/Privacy Act Officer
Small Business Administration
Washington, DC 20416

## SOCIAL SECURITY ADMINISTRATION

Mr. Gilbert C. Fisher (301) 934-1988
Director, Office of Information
Room 124, Altmeyer Bldg.
6401 Security Blvd.
Baltimore, MD 21235

## STATE DEPARTMENT

Mr. Frank M. Machak (202) 632-3411
Information & Privacy Coordinator
Room 1239
Bureau of Administration
Department of State
2201 C St., N.W.
Washington, DC 20520

Mr. Ely Maurer (202) 632-2682
Assistant Legal Advisor
Department of State
Washington, DC 20520

## TENNESSEE VALLEY AUTHORITY

Mr. Justin M. Schwamm, Sr. (615) 852-2361
Assistant General Counsel
400 Commerce Ave.
Tennessee Valley Authority
Knoxville, TN 37902

## TRANSPORTATION DEPARTMENT

Ms. Rebecca L. Dailey (202) 426-4542
FOIA Office
Office of Public Affairs
Washington, DC 20590

Mr. Gregory D. Wolfe (202) 426-4710
Attorney/Advisor
Office of the General Counsel
Department of Transportation
400 Seventh Street, S.W.
Washington, DC 20590

## TREASURY DEPARTMENT

Disclosure Branch (202) 566-5573
Information Services Division
Room 1322, Main Treasury
1500 Pennsylvania Ave., N.W.
Washington, DC 20220

Mr. Ronald Levy (202) 566-2327
Attorney/Advisor - FOIA
Department of the Treasury
Room 1409, Main Treasury
Washington, DC 20220

## U.S. INTERNATIONAL TRADE COMMISSION

Mr. Kenneth R. Mason (202) 523-0161
Secretary
U.S. International Trade Commission
701 E St., N.W.
Washington, DC 20436

Mr. W. W. Gearhart (202) 523-0379
Attorney/Advisor
Office of the General Counsel
U.S. International Trade Commission
701 E St., N.W.
Washington, DC 20436

## VETERANS ADMINISTRATION

Ms. Maureen Dinunzio (202) 389-3616
Director, Management Services
810 Vermont Ave., N.W.
Washington, DC 20420

Mr. Howard Lem (202) 389-3431
Staff Attorney
Office of General Counsel
810 Vermont Ave., N.W.
Washington, DC 20420

## THE WHITE HOUSE

General Counsel (202) 456-6640
Office of Administration
The White House Office
1600 Pennsylvania Ave., N.W.
Washington, DC 20500

## PUBLIC INFORMATION OFFICES

### ACTION
806 Connecticut Ave., N.W.
Washington, DC 20525
(202) 254-6886

### ADMINISTRATIVE OFFICE OF U.S. COURTS
Washington, DC 20544
(202) 633-6097

### AGRICULTURE DEPARTMENT
14 St. & Independence Ave., S.W.
Washington, DC 20250
(202) 447-2791

### AIR FORCE DEPARTMENT
See Defense Department below.

### ARMY DEPARTMENT
See Defense Department below.

### CIVIL AERONAUTICS BOARD
1825 Connecticut Avenue, N.W.
Washington, DC 20428
(202) 673-5990

### CIVIL RIGHTS COMMISSION
1121 Vermont Avenue, N.W.
Washington, DC 20425
(202) 254-6697

### CIVIL SERVICE COMMISSION
See Office of Personnel Management below.

### COAST GUARD
400 7th Street, S.W.
Washington, DC 30590
(202) 426-2158

### COMMERCE DEPARTMENT
14th St. and Constitution Ave., N.W.
Washington, DC 20230
(202) 377-2000

### COMMODITY FUTURES TRADING COMMISSION
2033 K Street, N.W.
Washington, DC 20581
(202) 254-8630

### CONSUMER PRODUCT SAFETY COMMISSION
1111 18th Street, N.W.
Washington, DC 20207
(202) 634-7780

### COPYRIGHT OFFICE (Library of Congress)
James Madison Memorial Building
101 Independence Avenue, S.E.
Washington, DC 20540
(202) 287-8700

### COURTS
See Judicial Branch above.

### DEFENSE DEPARTMENT
The Pentagon
Washington, DC 20301
(202) 545-6700

**Department of Air Force**
The Pentagon
Washington, DC 20330
(202) 695-2246

**Department of Army**
The Pentagon
Washington, DC 20310
(202) 697-7589

**Department of Navy**
The Pentagon
Washington, DC 20350
(202) 695-0965

**U.S. Marine Corps**
Arlington Annex
Arlington, VA 20380
(202) 694-2958

## DRUG ENFORCEMENT ADMINISTRATION
See Justice Department below.

## EDUCATION, DEPARTMENT OF
400 Maryland Avenue, S.W.
Washington, DC 20201
The Department of Education was established on October 17, 1979. On that date the Department of Health, Education & Welfare ceased to exist, with its functions taken up by the Department of Education and the Department of Health and Human Services (see below).

## EMPLOYEES COMPENSATION & SECURITY BUREAU
See Labor Department (Employment Standards), below.

## ENERGY DEPARTMENT
Forrestal Building
1000 Independence Avenue, S.W.
Washington, DC 20585
(202) 252-5565

## ENVIRONMENTAL PROTECTION AGENCY
401 M Street, S.W.
Washington, DC 20460
(202) 755-0707

## EQUAL EMPLOYMENT OPPORTUNITY COMMISSION
2401 E Street, N.W.
Washington, DC 20506
(202) 634-6930

## FEDERAL CONTRACT COMPLIANCE OFFICE
See Labor Department below.

## FEDERAL DEPOSIT INSURANCE CORPORATION
550 17th Street, N.W.
Washington, DC 20429
(202) 389-4221

## FEDERAL ELECTION COMMISSION
1325 K Street, N.W.
Washington, DC 20463
Information on federal political fundraising laws
DC Metropolitan Area......(202) 523-4068
Other US................(800) 424-9530

## FEDERAL ENERGY REGULATORY COMMISSION
**(Department of Energy)**
825 North Capitol Street
Washington, DC 20426
(202) 357-8380

## FEDERAL HIGHWAY ADMINISTRATION
See Department of Transportation below.

## FEDERAL HOME LOAN BANK BOARD
320 First Street, N.W.
Washington, DC 20552
(202) 377-6000

## FEDERAL JUDICIAL CENTER
Dolly Madison House
1520 H Street, N.W.
Washington, DC 20005
(202) 633-6311

## FEDERAL LABOR RELATIONS AUTHORITY
1900 E Street, N.W.
Washington, DC 20424
(202) 632-4524

## FEDERAL MARITIME COMMISSION
1100 L Street, N.W.
Washington, DC 20573
(202) 523-5707

## FEDERAL MEDIATION & CONCILIATION SERVICE
2100 K Street, N.W.
Washington, DC 20427
(202) 653-5280

## FEDERAL MINE SAFETY & HEALTH REVIEW COMMISSION
1730 K Street, N.W.
Washington, DC 20006
(202) 653-5633

## FEDERAL REGISTER
General Services Administration
Washington, DC 20408
(202) 523-5240

## FEDERAL RESERVE SYSTEM
20th St. & Constitution Ave., N.W.
Washington, DC 20551
(202) 452-3204

## EXPORT-IMPORT BANK
811 Vermont Avenue, N.W.
Washington, DC 20571
(202) 566-8990

## FEDERAL AVIATION ADMINISTRATION
See Department of Transportation below.

## FEDERAL BUREAU OF INVESTIGATION
See Justice Department below.

**FEDERAL COMMUNICATIONS
    COMMISSION**
1919 M Street, N.W.
Washington, DC 20554
(202) 254-7674

**FEDERAL TRADE COMMISSION**
Pennsylvania Avenue & Sixth Street, N.W.
Washington, DC 20580
(202) 523-3830

**FISH & WILDLIFE SERVICE**
See Interior Department below.

**FOOD & DRUG ADMINISTRATION**
**(Department of Health and Human Services)**
5600 Fishers Lane
Rockville, MD 20852
(301) 443-4177

**FOREST SERVICE**
See Agriculture Department above.

**GENERAL ACCOUNTING OFFICE**
441 G Street, N.W.
Washington, DC
(202) 275-2812

**GENERAL SERVICES ADMINISTRATION**
18th & F Streets, N.W. (GSA Building)
Washington, DC 20405
(202) 566-1231

**GEOLOGICAL SURVEY**
**(Interior Department)**
12201 Sunrise Valley Drive
Reston, VA 22092
(703) 860-7444

**GOVERNMENT PRINTING OFFICE
GPO BOOKSTORE**
Washington, DC
(202) 275-2091

**HEALTH AND HUMAN SERVICES**
200 Independence Avenue, S.W.
Washington, DC 20201
(202) 245-6343

**DEPARTMENT OF HOUSING & URBAN
    DEVELOPMENT**
451 Seventh Street, S.W.
Washington, DC 20410
(202) 755-6420

*IMMIGRATION & NATURALIZATION
    SERVICE*
*(Justice Department)*
425 I Street, N.W.
Washington, DC 20536
(202) 633-2000

**INTERIOR DEPARTMENT**
18th & C Streets, N.W.
Washington, DC 20240
(202) 343-3171

**INTERNAL REVENUE SERVICE**
1111 Constitution Avenue, N.W.
Washington, DC 20224
(202) 566-4743
For general assistance and problem
resolution, consult white pages of your
telephone directory for local IRS office.

**INTERNATIONAL COMMUNICATIONS
AGENCY**
1750 Pennsylvania Avenue, N.W.
Washington, DC 20547
(202) 724-9103

**INTERNATIONAL DEVELOPMENT
    COOPERATION AGENCY**
Department of State Building
320 21st Street, N.W.
Washington, DC 20523
(202) 632-8150

**INTERNATIONAL TRADE COMMISSION**
701 E Street, N.W.
Washington, DC 20436
(202) 523-0161

**INTERSTATE COMMERCE COMMISSION**
12th Street & Constitution Avenue, N.W.
Washington, DC 20423
(202) 275-7252

**JUDICIAL PANEL ON MULTIDISTRICT
    LITIGATION**
1030 Fifteenth Street, N.W.
Washington, DC 20005
(202) 653-6090

**JUSTICE DEPARTMENT**
10th Street & Constitution Avenue, N.W.
Washington, DC 20530
(202) 633-2007

**LABOR DEPARTMENT**
200 Constitution Avenue, N.W.
Washington, DC 20210
(202) 523-7316

**LEGAL SERVICES CORPORATION**
733 15th Street, N.W.
Washington, DC 20005
(202) 272-4030

**LIBRARY OF CONGRESS**
First Street & Independence Avenue, S.E.
Washington, DC 20540
(202) 287-5000

**MARINE CORPS**
See Defense Department above.

**NATIONAL AERONAUTICS & SPACE ADMINISTRATION (NASA)**
400 Maryland Avenue, S.W.
Washington, DC 20546
(202) 755-8341

**NATIONAL ARCHIVES & RECORD SERVICE (GSA)**
Pennsylvania Avenue & 8th Street, N.W.
Washington, DC 20408
(202) 523-3099

**NATIONAL FOUNDATION ON THE ARTS & HUMANITIES**
**National Endowment for the Arts**
2401 E Street, N.W.
Washington, D.C. 20506
(202) 634-6369
**National Endowment for the Humanities**
806 15th Street, N.W.
Washington, D.C. 20506
(202) 724-0386

**NATIONAL HIGHWAY TRAFFIC SAFETY**
(also see Transportation Department below)
**Toll Free Auto Safety Hotline**
    District of Columbia . . . . . . (202) 426-012:
    Other Continental US . . . . (800) 424-939:

**NATIONAL LABOR RELATIONS BOARD**
1717 Pennsylvania Avenue, N.W.
Washington, DC 20570
(202) 632-4950

**NATIONAL MEDIATION BOARD**
1425 K Street, N.W.
Washington, DC 20572
(202) 523-5920

**NATIONAL PARK SERVICE**
(Interior Department)
Department of Interior
Washington, DC 20240
(202) 343-7349

**NATIONAL SCIENCE FOUNDATION**
1800 G Street, N.W.
Washington, DC 20550
(202) 357-9498

**NATIONAL TECHNICAL INFORMATION SERVICE**
Department of Commerce
5285 Port Royal Road
Springfield, VA 22161
(703) 487-4600

**NATIONAL TRANSPORTATION SAFETY BOARD**
800 Independence Avenue, S.W.
Washington, DC 20594
(202) 382-6600

**NUCLEAR REGULATORY COMMISSION**
1717 H Street, N.W.
Washington, DC 20555
(202) 492-7715

**OCCUPATIONAL SAFETY & HEALTH ADMINISTRATION**
(Labor Department)
200 Constitution Avenue, N.W.
Washington, DC 20210
(202) 523-6091

**OCCUPATIONAL SAFETY & HEALTH REVIEW COMMISSION**
1825 K Street, N.W.
Washington, DC 20006
(202) 634-7991

**OFFICE OF PERSONNEL MANAGEMENT**
(Formerly known as Civil Service Commission)
1900 E Street, N.W.
Washington, DC 20415
(202) 632-5491

**PASSPORT OFFICE**
(State Department)
1425 K Street, N.W.
Washington, DC 20005
(202) 557-8200 (Washington, DC, area)
(202) 783-8170 (other areas)

**PATENT & TRADEMARK OFFICE**
(Commerce Department)
Department of Commerce Building
Washington, DC 20231
(703) 557-3080 (patent information)
(703) 557-3268 (trademark information)

**PEACE CORPS**
See ACTION above.

**PENNSYLVANIA AVENUE DEVELOPMENT CORPORATION**
425 13th Street, N.W.
Washington, DC 20004
(202) 566-0402

**PENSION BENEFIT GUARANTY CORPORATION**
2020 K Street, N.W.
Washington, DC 20006
(202) 254-4778

**POSTAL RATE COMMISSION**
2000 L Street, N.W.
Washington, DC 20268
(202) 254-3828

**POSTAL SERVICE, U.S.**
475 L'Enfant Plaza West, S.W.
Washington, DC 20260
(202) 245-4034

**SECURITIES & EXCHANGE
COMMISSION**
500 North Capitol Street
Washington, DC 20549
(202) 272-2650

**SELECTIVE SERVICE SYSTEM**
1023 31st Street, N.W.
Washington, DC 20435
(202) 724-0424

**SMALL BUSINESS ADMINISTRATION**
1441 L Street, N.W.
Washington, DC 20416
(202) 653-6823

**SMITHSONIAN INSTITUTION**
1000 Jefferson Drive, S.W.
Washington, DC 20560
(202) 357-1300

**SOCIAL SECURITY ADMINISTRATION**
Baltimore, MD 21235
(202) 594-1992

**TENNESSEE VALLEY AUTHORITY**
Knoxville Office Complex
400 Commerce Complex
Knoxville, TN 37901
(202) 623-3974

**STATE DEPARTMENT**
2201 C Street, N.W.
Washington, DC 20520
(202) 632-6575

**SUPREME COURT OF UNITED STATES**
See Judicial Branch above.

**TRADEMARK OFFICE
(Commerce Department)**
Department of Commerce
Washington, DC 20231
(703) 557-3268

**DEPARTMENT OF TRANSPORTATION**
400 7th Street, S.W.
Washington, DC 20590
(202) 426-4321

**Federal Aviation Administration**
800 Independence Avenue, S.W.
Washington, DC 20591
(202) 426-3883

**Federal Highway Administration**
400 7th Street, S.W.
Washington, DC 20591
(202) 426-0660

**Federal Railroad Administration**
400 7th Street, S.W.
Washington, DC 20590
(202) 426-0881

**National Highway Safety Administration**
400 7th Street, S.W.
Washington, DC 20590
(202) 426-9550

**Urban Mass Transportation Administration**
400 7th Street, S.W.
Washington, DC 20590
(202) 426-4043

**TREASURY DEPARTMENT**
15th Street & Pennsylvania Avenue, N.W.
Washington, DC 20220
(202) 566-2041

**URBAN MASS TRANSPORTATION
ADMINISTRATION**
See Department of Transportation above.

**VETERANS ADMINISTRATION**
810 Vermont Avenue, N.W.
Washington, DC 20420
(202) 275-1300

**VISA Information**
See State Department above.

**WATER RESOURCES COUNCIL**
2120 L Street, N.W.
Washington, DC 20037
(202) 254-8290

# RECENT FOIA REQUESTS

This section contains a specially-prepared listing that surveys Freedom of Information Act requests that have recently been submitted to major federal departments and agencies as indicated below. Included for each item are: material requested, name of the requestor, and agency response (when available). FOIA telephone numbers are also given. (For comprehensive FOIA/Privacy Act telephone directory, see section beginning on page 30.) The dates given are for the year 1981 unless otherwise indicated.

The intention here is to provide an indication of the range of material being requested under the Freedom of Information Act, and how the agencies are responding thereto. Most of the FOIA requests listed below were submitted by law firms, principally on behalf of their corporate clients.

The reader may find certain requests of particular interest and submit his own FOIA request for the material released to the original requestor; or he may want to contact the requestor directly.

Appendix C contains the full-text of several recent FOIA requests submitted to the Federal Trade Commission. Appendix D contains a federal court complaint, challenging the denial of an FOIA request.

## Antitrust Division, Justice Department
FOIA Office: (202) 633-2692

Documents re Justice Dep't (Antitrust Div.) investigation of monopolistic practices in beef industry. Req. by: Graham Purcell, Esq., of Purcell, Hanse & Henderson, Washington, D.C. Granted in part. 3/26. Exemptions: (b)(4), trade secrets; (b)(5), inter-intra agency memoranda; et al.

Dep't of Justice (Antitrust Div.) enforcement intentions re proposed joint venture involving acquisition and feeding of cattle by feedlots owned by Schaake, Van de Graaf & Monson. Req. by: Edwin H. Pewett, Esq., of Glassie, Pewett et al, Washington, D.C. Granted. 3/25.

Documents re operations of United Fruit, United Brands and Del Monte Corp. in Guatemala. Req. by: Herbert Berkson, Esq., Boston, Mass. Granted in part. 3/17. Exemptions: (b)(5), inter-intra agency memoranda; (b)(7)(D), confidential source.

Material re Justice Dep't (Antitrust Div.) investigations into following companies: Celanese, Shell Oil, Allied Chemical, Hercules, and Am. Cyanamid. Req. by: Michael Gottsegen, Esq., Environmental Action Foundation, Washington, D.C. Granted. 3/17.

Memo re Dep't of Justice investigation of Alcan's attempted purchase of Scottsboro smelter of Revere Copper Brass Inc. Req. by: Mr. R. Zurawski, of Woods Gordon Management Consultants, Winnipeg, Canada. Granted in part. 3/10. Exemptions: (b)(4), trade secrets; (b)(5), inter-intra agency memoranda; et al.

Records re 1969 grand jury investigation of quicklime industry, specifically recommendation of grand jury that investigation be closed without indictment. Req. by: Michael C. Cesarano, Esq., of Mershon, Sawyer et al, Miami, Fla. Granted. 3/10.

Previously released information re Remington Arms Co. Req. by: Fred D. Turnage, Esq., of Cleary, Gottlieb et al, Washington, D.C. Granted. 3/10.

Information re proposed merger of Columbia Pictures Industries Inc. and Metro-Goldwyn-Mayer Film Corp. (DOJ #60-6-037-22). Req. by: Carol S. Medelsohn, Esq., of Wyman, Bautzer et al, Washington, D.C. Granted. 3/10.

Copy of joint operating agreement and related documents re St. Louis Post-Dispatch and St. Louis Globe-Democrat. Req. by: Mr. Charles L. Klotzer, St. Louis Journalism Review, St. Louis, Mo. Granted. 3/6.

Information re Dep't of Justice (Antitrust Div.) investigation of retail milk prices in Southern California between 1970 and 1976. Req. by: Mark H. Penskar, Esq., of Pillsbury, Madison & Sutro, San Francisco, Calif. Granted in part. 3/5. Exemptions: (b)(3), specifically exempted by statute; (b)(5), inter-intra agency memoranda; et al.

Dep't of Justice files re pricing and competition in domestic aluminum industry. Req. by: Abraham N. Goldman, Esq., of Sheele, Serkland & Boyle, Chicago, Ill. Granted in part. 3/4. Exemptions: (b)(4), trade secrets; (b)(7)(A), enforcement proceedings; et al.

Access to Antitrust Div. records re post-tensioning industry.  Req. by:
Gordon Weinberg, Esq., of Sonenshine & Zipser, Los Angeles, Calif.  Granted
in part.  2/24.  Exemption: (b)(7)(D), confidential source.

Documents re investigations or proceedings conducted by Justice Dep't
(Antitrust Div.) concerning Tandy Corp., Radio Shack, Allied Radio Shack, A&A
Trading Co., or General Research of Electroncis Inc.  Req. by: Andrew B.
Melnick, Esq., of Weil, Gotschal & Manges, New York, N.Y.  Granted in part.
2/23.  Exemptions: (b)(5), inter-intra agency memoranda; (b)(7)(A), enforcement
proceedings; et al.

Previously released information re pricing practices of ready-mix concrete
suppliers in Cuyahoga, Western, and Geauga Counties, Ohio.  Req. by: Barbara
J. Bergeson, of Thompson, Hine & Flory, Washington, D.C.  Granted.  2/20.

Correspondence between Bechtel Corp. and Departments of Justice and State
re "U.S. v. Bechtel Corp.", Civil No.  C-76-99, Northern District of Georgia.
Req. by: Mr. Richard T. Cooper, Los Angeles Times, Washington, D.C.  Denied.
2/20.  Exemption: (b)(7)(A), enforcement proceedings.

Information re alleged bid-rigging activities in post-tension concrete
construction industry in United States.  Req. by: Donald G. Rez, Esq., of
Sullivan, Jones & Archer, San Diego, Calif.  Granted in part.  2/18.  Exemptions:
(b)(7)(A), enforcement proceedings; (b)(5), inter-intra agency memoranda; et al.

Previously released information as to whether thrift institutions should be
considered in defining relevant lines of commerce re analyzing effects on
competition in mergers, acquisitions or other combinations involving banks or
bank holding companies.  Req. by: Theresa A. Einhorn, Esq., of Zimmer & Einhorn,
Washington, D.C.  Granted.  2/4.

Records re: Amerco Inc., U-Haul Int'l Inc., their subsidiaries, affiliates
and other related companies of U-Haul family.  Req. by: Alan L. Moore, Esq., of
Gilbert & Moore.  Granted.  12/19/80.

Documents re acquisition of Courter Inc. by Bendix Corp.  Req. by: Mark
Mlotek, Esq., of Kaye, Scholer et al, New York, N.Y.  Granted.  12/19/80.

Documents re Swedish Match Co. (UMC Industries Inc.).  Req. by: Paul D.
Mannina, Esq., of Howrey & Simon, Washington, D.C.  Granted.  12/18/80.

Previously released information re issues affecting deregulation of motor
carrier industry.  Req. by: James A.  Calderwood, Esq., of Grave, Jaskiewicz et
al, Washington, D.C.  Granted.  12/16/80.

Consent decrees entered into between Dep't of Justice and ABC or Spelling-
Goldberg Inc.  Req. by: Fay Clayton, of Sachnoff, Schrager et al, Chicago, Ill.
Granted.  12/16/80.

Previously released informaltion re merger between LTV Corp. and Lykes Corp.
Req. by: Richard D. Greenfield, Esq., of Greenfield & Shoen, Bala Cynwyd, Pa.
Granted.  12/9/80.

**Consumer Product Safety Commission**
FOIA Office: (301) 492-6800

Information re recall of furnaces from March through May, 1978. Req. by: Bruce R. Schmidt, Asst. Attorney General, Buffalo, N.Y. Granted. 3/20.

Report re injuries associated with public playgrounds. Req. by: Stephen D. Bodman, Esq., of Langerman, Begman et al, Phoenix, Ariz. Granted. 3/19.

Computer printout re injuries associated with carbonated soft drink bottles. Req. by: Ms. Marielle M. Hoffman, of Morgan, Lewis & Bockius, Washington, D.C. Granted. 3/19.

Report entitled "Hazard Analysis on Contact Adhesive Fires." Req. by: H. James Tuchscherer, Esq., of Chambers, Nash et al, Wisconsin Rapids, Wisc. Granted. 3/18.

CPSC file re injuries associated with asbestos. Req. by: Robert C. Peach, Esq., of Peach, Shapiro & Peach, San Bernardino, Calif. Granted. 3/18.

Material re hazards associated with urea foam insulation. Req. by: Robert E. Paul, Esq., of Shein & Brookman, Philadelphia, Pa. Granted. 3/16.

Information re sulfuric acid drain cleaners. Req. by: Richard L. Anderson, Esq., of Gibson & Anderson, Kimberling City, Mo. Granted. 3/16.

CPSC file re White-Rogers/Emerson Electric Thermostats. Req. by: Stanley E. Karon, Esq., of Robins, Zelle et al, St. Paul, Minn. Granted. 3/16.

Report on Ladder Testing Standard. Req. by: Scott Melton, Esq., of Conte & Courtney, Conway, Pa. Granted. 3/16.

Information re swimming pool slide accidents. Req. by: Joseph M. Brown, Jr., Cunningham, Bounds et al, Mobile, Ala. Granted. 3/16.

Material re automatic drip coffeemakers and thermal cutoff devices. Req. by: Holly E. Leese, Esq., of Fitzgerald, Young & Peters, Detroit, Mich. Granted in part. 3/13. Exemption: (b)(4), trade secrets.

Information re 3M Fast Bond 10 Contact Cement. Req. by: Randa M. Owen, Esq., of Parker, Johnson et al, Orlando, Fla. Granted. 3/13.

Safety data re hot water heaters. Req. by: Ms. Lynn Nelson, of Fulbright & Jaworski, Houston, Tex. Granted. 3/13.

CPSC - promulgated safety standards re walk-behind lawn mowers. Req. by: Mr. Randall Skiles, Stern Law Office, Madison, Wisc. Granted. 3/13.

Accident reports re infant swings. Req. by: Morton A. Schwab, Esq., of Schneider, Kleimick et al, New York, N.Y. Granted. 3/13.

Records re special packaging provisions of Poison Prevention Packaging Act. Req. by: Gordon Rousseau, Esq., Law Offices of Lawrence W. Bierlein, Washington, D.C. Granted. 3/12.

Consumer complaint and investigation report on Century Super Coupe regarding baby walker. Req. by: Aaron Locker, Esq., of Locker & Greenburg, New York, N.Y. Granted. 3/11.

Report on Nike Roadrunner Shoes. Req. by: Gregory T. Chestnut, Esq., Office of the Attorney General, Columbia, S.C. Granted in part. 2/20. Exemption: (b)(3), specifically exempted by statute.

Accident report re power lawn mower known as "Chieftain." Req. by: Charles A. Zahn, Esq., of Golden, Shore et al, South River, N.J. Granted. 2/20.

Information re aluminum baseball bats with rubber grips. Req. by: Richard E. McGreevy, Esq., Law Offices of Richard B. Barrett, Burlingame, Calif. Granted. 2/20.

Report entitled "Feasibility of Lowering Water Heater Temperature as a Means of Reducing Scald Hazards," prepared by Arthur D. Little Inc., Jan. 1977. Req. by: Mr. Ronald W. Horgan, John M. Norman Inc., Oklahoam City, Okla. Granted. 2/27.

Information on Homelite XL-12 chain saws. Req. by: Robert G. Kerrigan, Esq., of Kerrigan, Estess & Rankin, Pensacola, Fla. Granted. 2/6.

Documents re burning behavior of upholstered chairs and mattresses. Req. by: William A. Posey, Esq., of Keeting, Muething & Klekamp, Cincinnati, Ohio. Granted. 2/17.

Accident reports re cigarette lighters. Req. by: Mr. Patrick J. Dexter, Gillette Medical Evaluation Labs, Rockville, Md. Granted. 2/17.

Copy of CPSC annual report on Administration of Freedom of Information Act, 1979. Req. by: Mr. Samuel Cohen, Legal Research Librarian, New York, N.Y. Granted. 2/17.

Log of meeting on July 28, 1980, between CPSC staff and Japanese Kerosene Manufacturer Representatives. Req. by: Mr. Ching Tan, Jersey City, N.J. Granted. 2/18.

Briefing package re Aquaslide 'n' Dive Corp. petition to establish swimming pool slide standards. Req. by: James N. Sinunu, Esq., of Popelka, Allard et al, San Jose, Calif. Granted. 2/20.

Computer printout of incidents involving gas-fired furnaces. Req. by: Paul J. Doesschate, Esq., of Hoge, Fenton et al, San Jose, Calif. Granted. 2/9.

Consumer complaints re pressure cookers. Req. by: Mark Glass, Esq., of Cohn, Carr et al, East St. Louis, Mo. Granted. 2/6.

Petition asking that CPSC set standards for football helmets and shoes and Federal Register Notice re denial as to football shoes. Req. by: Richard J. Carroll, Esq., of Carroll, Panepinto et al, Jersey City, N.J. Granted. 2/13.

CPSC economic and environmental analysis re refuse bins. Req. by: Howard Lightman, Esq., of Newton & Jennings, North Weymouth, Mass. Granted. 2/13.

Information re explosions in carbonated soda bottles. Req. by: Thomas D. Burkhart, Esq., Law Firm of Jerome E. Burns, Saginaw, Mich. Granted. 2/13.

Accident reports re fire extinguishers. Req. by: W.S. Pritchard, Esq., of Pritchard, McCall et al, Birmingham, Ala. Granted. 2/6.

Information re malfunctions associated with General Elec. Alarm Clock. Req. by: Robert L. Hersh, Esq., San Anselmo, Calif. Granted. 2/9.

Documents re Bombardier Ltd. Req. by: Donald L. Morgan, Esq., of Cleary, Gottlieb et al, Washington, D.C. Granted. 2/11.

Consumer complaints re hydraulic wood splitters. Req. by: Stephen D. Willett, Esq., of Olson & Willett, Phillips, Wisc. Granted. 2/11.

Documents re accident associated with amusement ride "Willard's Whizzer" of Marriott's "Great America" theme ride at Santa Clara, Calif. Req. by: William A. Jennings, Esq., of San Jose, Calif. Granted. 2/13.

Briefing package on chain saws. Req. by: H. Douglas Brand, Esq., of Walz, Fershee et al, Big Rapids, Mich. Granted. 2/13.

Information re health effects of formaldehyde. Req. by: David Collins, Esq., of Collins & Grimm, Macon, Ga. Granted. 2/13.

Documents re dual purpose packaging. Req. by: Sarah W. Hays, Esq., of Gage & Tucker, Kansas City, Mo. Granted in part. 2/4. Exemption: (b)(4), trade secrets.

Documents re hazards associated with hot tubs. Req. by: Edward F. Morgan, Esq., Tuscaloosa, Ala. Granted. 1/13.

CPSC files re Cell-U-Save Inc. Req. by: William H. Heritage, Jr., Esq., of Landman, Luyendyk et al, Grand Rapids, Mich. Granted. 1/9.

Information re Okla Homer Smith cribs. Req. by: James R. Treese, Esq., of Stoner, Treese et al, Washington, D.C. Granted in part. 1/8. Exemption: (b)(4), trade secrets.

Report on Chronic Health Effects of Formaldehyde, dated 11/21/80. Req. by: David W. Coody, Esq., of Minton, Burton & Fitzgerald, Austin, Tex. Granted. 1/7.

Hazards associated with refuse bins. Req. by: Donald C. McCabe, Esq., Law Office of Nomberg & McCabe, Daleville, Ala. Granted. 1/7.

Investigative file on recessed lighting fixtures. Req. by: Mark Cassidy, Esq., Office of the Attorney General, Spokane, Wash. Granted. 1/5.

Safety data re Montgomery Ward color televisions. Req. by: Howard E. Lowe, Esq., Los Angeles, Calif. Granted. 1/23.

Information re Frigidaire refrigerators. Req. by: John E. Trojack, Esq., of Wagner, Rutchick et al, St. Paul, Minn. Granted. 1/23.

CPSC investigative reports re Hobart Corp. Req. by: Thomas H. Rogers, Legal Dep't, Hobart Corp., Troy, Ohio. Granted. 1/19.

Feasibility study for CB and Antenna Safety Standard. Req. by: Ronald Zappelli, Esq., Pacific Gas & Elec. Co., San Francisco, Calif. Granted. 1/19.

Information re Mattel Co. Req. by: Steven R. Pruzan, Esq., of Miracle, Pruzan & Nelson, Seattle, Wash. Granted. 1/28.

Documents re use of formaldehyde in consumer products. Req. by: Richard W. Moore, Esq., of Sherling, Drinkard & Moore, Mobile, Ala. Granted. 1/27.

CPSC briefing package re chain saw injuries from kickback. Req. by: John P. Liekar, Jr., Esq., Law Offices of Michael E. Kusturiss, Canonsburg, Pa. Granted. 1/26.

Information re J.C. Penny Wetcell Batteries. Req. by: Ms. Joyce H. Wall, of Leitner, Warner et al, Chattanooga, Tenn. Granted. 1/26.

Documents re shock hazards associated with "Trouble Lights." Req. by: Craig A. Levien, Esq., of Betty, Newman et al, Davenport, Iowa. Granted. 1/23.

Information re Amana Microwave Ovens. Req. by: Dennis A. Vanderberg, Esq., of Pyszka, Kessler et al, Miami, Fla. Granted. 1/23.

Hazard analysis on bottles for carbonated soft drinks. Req. by: Jerome T. Murphy, Esq., Chicago, Ill. Granted. 1/23.

Injury information re MARX toy cars. Req. by: Thomas R. Downing, Esq., of Hardy & Wolfe, Lewistown, Me. Granted. 1/23.

Material re "Reach" toothbrushes. Req. by: Crawford Law Firm, Savannah, Ga. Granted. 12/30/80.

## Department of Energy
FOIA Office: (202) 252-5965

Response of Tesoro Petroleum Co. to Notice of Probable Violation filed by San Antonio, Tex., office of DOE. Req. by: William G. Carpenter, Esq., of Cable, McDaniel et al, Baltimore, Md. Granted. 2/17.

DOE's comments on GAO Report issued May 29, 1979, entitled "Improvements Needed in Enforcement of Crude Oil Reseller Price Controls." Req. by: Jacob Dweck, Esq., of Ginsburg, Feldman et al, Washington, D.C. Granted in part. 2/17. Exemption: (b)(5), inter-intra agency memoranda.

Materials contained in two administrative complaints filed by Boscobel Oil Co. against ARCO. Req. by: Mr. Victor P. Haley, of Arnold & Porter, Washington, D.C. Granted in part. 2/13. Exemption: (b)(4), trade secrets.

Draft Notice of Probable Violation to Standard Oil of Indiana re their class of purchaser and supporting exhibits. Req. by: Robert J. Hennessey, Esq., of Larkin, Hoffman et al, Minneapolis, Minn. Granted in part. 2/13. Exemption: (b)(5), inter-intra agency memoranda.

Previously released information re definition and interpretation of "exchange," "matching purpose and sale transaction," and "layering." Req. by: Warren E. Connelly, Esq., of Akin, Gump et al, Washington, D.C. Granted. 2/12.

Copy of FY 1980-1987 Telecommunications Long Range Plan dated Dec. 16, 1980. Req. by: Ms. Wanda Ramsey Glanzman, GTE Service, Corp., Washington, D.C. Granted. 2/24.

Original and various revisions of DOE Enforcement Manual dealing with §4.702.02(E) and §4.702.03, specifically re nonproduct cost increases. Req. by: Alfred R. Hupp, Jr., Esq., of Lathrop, Koontz et al, Kansas City, Mo. Granted. 2/24.

Copy of GAO Report dated May 29, 1979, entitled "Improvements Needed in Enforcement of Crude Oil Reseller Price Controls," Req. by: Joe A. Rudberg, Esq., of Thompson & Knight, Dallas, Tex. Granted. 2/13.

Article on Statute of Limitations Defense in DOE Enforcement Actions prepared by David J. Beck, Esq., of Law Firm of Fulbright & Jaworski. Req. by: Whayne C. Priest, Jr., Esq., of English, Lucas et al, Bowling Green, Ky. Granted in part. 2/4. Exemption: (b)(5), inter-intra agency memoranda.

List of cases of computer crime and computer abuse involving the DOE since 1977. Req. by: Ms. Suzanne St. Pierre, CBS News, Washington, D.C. Granted in part. 2/3. Exemption: (b)(7)(A), enforcement proceedings.

Data which could be used to establish market prices for butane and propane sold by resellers during period from November 1973 through June 1976 in certain areas in northern California. Req. by: James P. Lough, Esq., of Borton, Petrini & Conron, Bakersfield, Calif. Granted. 1/30.

Documents interpreting whether undercharges on sales of crude oil may be offset against overcharges on sales of crude oil to same purchasers where such undercharges result from misapplication of the property concept. Req. by: Jacob Dweck, Esq., of Ginsburg, Feldman et al, Washington, D.C. Granted. 1/29.

Copies of Consent Orders issued to crystal Oil Co., Newmont Oil Co., and Tipperary Oil & Gas Corp. Req. by: Mr. L.W. Smock, Mobil Oil Corp., Dallas, Tex. Granted. 1/29.

Letter sent by House (U.S. Congress) Energy & Power Subcommittee Chairman John Dingell to DOE Secretary Duncan on Dec. 29, 1980, re proposed settlement with Getty Oil Co. Req. by: Mr. John Laskey, of Steptoe & Johnson, Washington, D.C. Granted. 1/28.

Maximum and representative prices for reference crude oil for each month of the years 1977, 1978, and 1980. Req. by: Richard C. Morse, Esq., Atlantic Richfield Co., Los Angeles, Calif. Granted. 1/22.

Information re dumping of radioactive wastes off shores of California, Oregon or Washington. Req. by: Glen H. Spain, Esq., Lakespur, Calif. Granted. 1/20.

Copies of Proposed Remedial Orders (PRO) issued to Atlantic Richfield Co. on May 15, 1980, and Sept. 3, 1980. Req. by: W. Dennis Summers, Esq., of Hallman & Summers, Atlanta, Ga. Granted. 1/19.

Documents re issuance of Notice of Probable Violation (NOPV) to CIBRO Sales Corp. Req. by: William W. Scott, Esq., of Collier, Shannon et al, Washington, D.C. Granted. 1/19.

Copy of Consent Order issued to Gulf Corp. on Nov. 21, 1979. Req. by: Ms. Beth Ewing, of Sutherland, Asbill & Brennan, Washington, D.C. Granted. 1/15.

Proposed Order of Disallowance issued to Atlantic Richfield Co. in May 1980. Req. by: W. Dennis Summers, Esq., of Hallman & Summers, Atlanta, Ga. Granted. 1/15.

Documents re audits or investigations of Saber Petroleum concerning sales of No. 2 fuel oil during period Nov. 1, 1973, to Jan. 31, 1975. Req. by: Dillon Ferguson, Esq., of Butler, Binion et al, Washington, D.C. Granted in part. 1/14. Exemption: (b)(5), inter-intra agency memoranda.

Copies of all Notices of Probable Violations, Consent Orders, Proposed Remedial Orders, Final Remedial Orders, and Remedial Orders for Immediate Compliance issued to crude oil resellers since Jan. 1, 1974. Req. by: Alan L. Mintz, Esq., of Van Ness, Feldman & Sutcliffe, Washington, D.C. Granted. 1/12.

List of proposers for initial competition cycle for loan guarantees for alcohol fuel projects established under DOE's loan guarantee program for alcohol fuels, biomass energy and municipal waste energy projects. Req. by: Dennis J. Riley, Esq., of Batzell, Nunn & Bode, Washington, D.C. Granted. 1/9.

Notices of Probable Violation (NOPV) issued to Glenrock Refining on March 17, 1980, and Northland Oil & Refining on March 28, 1980, and the responses to those NOPVs. Req. by: Mitchell S. Dupler, Esq., of Cleary, Gottlieb et al, Washington, D.C. Granted. 1/9.

Previously released information re: meaning of "nearest comparable outlet" in 10 C.F.R. §212.111(b)(3), "improper certification" in §§212.131 and .185(c), "pooling" in 212.185(e), "practice" in §§205.202 and 210.62(c), and "layering" in §212.186. Req. by: Edward L. Rubinoff, Esq., of Akin, Gump et al, Washington, D.C. Granted. 1/7.

Material prepared by DOE re audits of and civil actions brought against major oil companies, particularly that which address the legality of DOE's discretion to authorize and implement procedures for distributing the remaining residual funds from a judgment or Consent order. Req. by: Steven E. Ferrey, Esq., Nat'l Consumer Law Center, Boston, Mass. Granted in part. 12/31/80. Exemptions: (b)(5), inter-intra agency memoranda; (b)(7)(A), enforcement proceedings.

Documents re DOE administrative charges filed against Hertz Rent-a-Car concerning refueling-fee overcharges. Req. by: John E. Grasberger, Esq., of Milberg, Weiss et al, San Diego, Calif. Granted in part. 12/29/80. Exemptions: (b)(4), trade secrets; (b)(7)(A), enforcement proceedings.

Previously released information re practice by crude oil resellers of "pooling" certifications covering crude oil. Req. by: Ms. Deborah G. Zimmerman, of Butler, Binion et al, Washington, D.C. Granted. 12/12/80.

List of electric powerplants that have filed for Special temporary Public Interest Exemptions from provisions of Fuel Use Act. Req. by: Mr. Frank Jacobs, Texas Oil & Gas Corp., Dallas, Tex. Granted. 12/18/80.

Records re DOE regulations on Residential Conservation Services (RCS) program, 10 CFR Part 456, specifically pertaining to urea-formaldehyde foam insulation material and formaldehyde gas. Req. by: Phillip D. Cameron, Esq., Worthington, Ohio. Granted. 12/17/80.

List of Permissible Average Markup (PAM) reported since Jan. 1980 by individual crude resellers for Northern Rocky Mountain Area. Req. by: Charles M. Seeger, Esq., of Nelson & Harding, Washington, D.C. Granted. 12/17/80.

**Environmental Protection Agency**
FOIA Office: (202) 755-2764

Copy of Cancer Assessment Group (CAG) "Preliminary Report on Population Risk to Arsenic Exposures." Req. by: Jessie M. Colgate, Esq., of Steptoe & Johnson, Washington, D.C. Granted. 3/25.

Cost-benefit and other economic studies by EPA re 50 PPM cutoff for the generation of PCB, used as basis for implementation of PCB Use Ban regulations under Sec. 6(e) of Toxic Substances Control Act. Req. by: Douglas M. Bagge, Esq., of Reid & Priest, New York, N.Y. Granted. 3/24.

Information re safe application of pesticide that goes under trade name "Baygon." Req. by: Ronald E. Dobelstein, Esq., of Krause, Reinhard & Pozen, Miami, Fla. Granted. 3/13.

Submissions by New York State re its efforts to obtain interim authorization for its hazardous waste program. Req. by: Robert G. Harvey, Esq., of Nixon, Hargrave et al, Rochester, N.Y. Granted. 3/2.

Information re penalty assessments for violations of inventory reporting regulations under Sec. 8(b) of Toxic Substances Control Act and relationship of these penalties to pre-manufacture notification penalties under Sec. 5 of Act. Req. by: Russel S. Frye, Esq., of Smith & Schnacke, Dayton, Ohio. Granted. 3/10.

Safety data re pesticide "Atrotol." Req. by: Martha Evans, Esq., of Johnson, Harrang et al, Eugene, Ore. Granted. 3/5.

Information re use by San Diego County of "Orthene" on tomato plants. Req. by: Jon D. Demorest, Esq., of Latham & Watkins, San Diego, Calif. Granted. 2/10.

Report entitled: "Fungicides: An Overivew of Their Significance to Agriculture and Their Pesticide Regulatory Implications." Req. by: Donna Diamond, of McKenna, Sellers & Cunio, Washington, D.C. Granted. 1/27.

Copies of all substantial risk notifications as per Sec. 8(e) of Toxic Substances Control Act for silicone and carbon black. Req. by: Marshall Lee Miller, Esq., of Peid & Priest, New York, N.Y. Granted. 1/23.

Documents used in establishing effluent limitation guidelines, new source performance standards, and pre-treatment standards for control of ammonia, chloroform, zinc, and other substances. Req. by: John N. Hanson, Esq., of Beveridge, Fairbanks & Diamond, Washington, D.C. Granted in part. 1/23. Exemption: (b)(4), trade secrets.

Reports prepared by META Systems Inc. in providing assistance to EPA re assessment of economic impact on proposed effluent limitation guidelines for Pulp, Paper & Paperboard Category (Dec. 1980). Req. by: John N. Hanson, Esq., of Beveridge, Fairbanks & Diamond, Washington, D.C. Granted in part. 2/5. Exemption: (b)(5), inter-intra agency memoranda.

Environmental compliance history of several companies, including Precision Minerals Inc., of Essex County, N.Y., Cominco American, of Beatrice, Neb., and other locations, and The Soo Line RR. Req. by: Thomas W. Brunner, Esq., of Wald, Harkrader & Ross, Washington, D.C. Granted. 1/29.

Administrative orders issued against Cannelton Industries Inc., West Virginia. Req. by: Robert P. Mollen, Esq., of Fried, Frank et al, Washington, D.C. Granted. 1/15.

Materials used in designating Pentachlorophenol as hazardous substance and determining the exportable quantity for it. Req. by: David Ludder, Esq., Asst. Attorney General, Montgomery, Ala. Granted. 1/14.

Petitions from Dresser Industries and John Deere Des Moines Works requesting EPA to delist as hazardous waste the sludges they generate. Req. by: Robert E. Lockner, Esq., of Ross, Hardies et al, Chicago, Ill. Granted. 1/15.

Documents re emission of pollutants from gas, oil, or solid fuel-fired central heating units for home or commercial use. Req. by: John D. McInerney, Esq., of Cleary, Gottlieb et al, Washington, D.C. Granted. 12/22/80.

## Federal Communications Commission
FOIA Office: (202) 632-7143

Copy of FCC 1973-74 investigation files re Station KPLM-TV, Palm Springs, Calif. Req. by: Ms. Susan Wing, of Hogan & Hartson, Washington, D.C. Granted in part. 4/10. Exemptions: (b)(5), inter-intra agency memoranda; (b)(7)(D), confidential source.

FCC files re Spanish Int'l Communications Corp. (SICC) and Television Station KMEX, Los Angeles, Calif. Req. by: Meyer S. Levitt, Esq., of Brown & Brown, Los Angeles, Calif. Granted in part. 4/2. Exemptions: (b)(4), trade secrets; (b)(7)(A), enforcement proceedings.

List of AM and FM stations which have filed for license renewal and whose renewal applications have petitions filed against them. Req. by: Robert J. O'Regan, Esq., Am. Legal Foundation, Washington, D.C. Granted. 3/9.

Information re any alleged unfair trade practices filed against Westinghouse Broadcasting Co. or its subsidiaries. Req. by: Martin R. Leader, Esq., of Fisher, Wayland et al, Washington, D.C. Granted. 2/26.

Documents re possible employment of FCC of outside consultants or contractors to aid the Common Carrier Bureau in CC Docket #80-633. Req. by: Alexander Humphrey, Esq., RCA Global Communications Inc., Washington, D.C. Granted in part. 2/13. Exemption: (b)(5), inter-intra agency memoranda.

## Federal Trade Commission
FOIA Office: (202) 523-3582

Report on real estate brokers which have been prepared by FTC Los Angeles Regional Office. 3/18. Req. by: Mr. Jeffrey A. Mills, Associated Press, Washington, D.C. Granted in part. 4/3. Exemptions: (b)(5), inter-intra agency memoranda; (b)(7)(A), enforcement proceedings.

Petitions filed by Johnson Products and Revlon Inc. re hair relaxer manufacturers. 3/16. Req. by: Eldon L. Wetmore, Esq., Tarrytown, N.Y. Granted. 4/3.

Information re synthetic hair or fiber implants. 3/9. Req. by: Michael J. Waldman, Esq., of Ferrara & Waldman, Cherry Hill, N.J. Granted in part. 4/10. Exemptions: (b)(4), trade secrets; (b)(5), inter-intra agency memoranda; (b)(7)(C), invasion of personal privacy; et al.

Documents re evaluation of FTC's investigation of lead antiknock industry. 3/11. Req. by: Allan J. Topol, Esq., of Covington & Burling, Washington, D.C. Granted in part. 4/8. Exemptions: (b)(5), inter-intra agency memoranda; (b)(7)(A), enforcement proceedings.

Consumer complaints re Champion Home Builder and/or Titan Homes Inc. 3/12. Req. by: Johnson S. Albright, Esq., of Albright, Degnan et al, West Henrietta, N.Y. Granted. 3/31.

Documents compiled by FTC re Gillette Co. which refer or relate to safety razor industry. 3/13. Req. by: Robert R. Salman, Esq., of Phillips, Nizer et al, New York, N.Y. Granted in part. 3/30. Exemptions: (b)(5), inter-intra agency memoranda; (b)(7)(A), enforcement proceedings.

Correspondence between FTC and Blow-Rite Insulation Co. 3/5. Req. by: Gerald E. Rosen, Esq., of Miller, Canfield et al, Detroit, Mich. Granted in part. 3/26. Exemptions: (b)(5), inter-intra agency memoranda; (b)(7)(A), enforcement proceedings.

Documents re FTC Docket No. C-2971, Fedders Corp. (heat pump problems).
3/6. Req. by: David H. Meginniss, Esq., of Hornsby, Blankenship et al,
Huntsville, Ala. Granted in part. 3/23. Exemptions: (b)(5), inter-intra
agency memoranda; (b)(7)(A), enforcement proceedings; et al.

Record re FTC and other investigations re Canadian Potash Industry. 3/3.
Req. by: Reed L. von Maur, Esq., of Arent, Fox et al, Washington, D.C. Granted
in part. 3/18. Exemptions: (b)(5), inter-intra agency memoranda; (b)(7)(A),
enforcement proceedings.

Information re FTC policy in regard to resale price maintenance. 3/2.
Req. by: William A. Quinlan, Esq., Annapolis, Md. Granted. 3/12.

Background information re FTC study of Life Insurance Industry. 3/5.
Req. by: Ms. Eileen M. Burke, of Katten, Muchin et al, Chicago, Ill. Granted
in part. 3/11. Exemptions: (b)(4), trade secrets; (b)(5), inter-intra
agency memoranda; et al.

Previously released information re Sears Muzzler Mufflers. 3/2. Req. by:
Marc L. Fleischaker, Esq., of Arent, Fox et al, Washington, D.C. Granted. 3/5.

Documents re FTC's investigation of Nat'l Revenue Corp. in connection with
compliance with Fair Debt Collection Practices Act. 2/26. Req. by: Robert
Disharoon, Esq., of Spridgen, Barrett et al, Santa Rosa, Calif. Granted in part.
4/2. Exemptions: (b)(4), trade secrets; (b)(7)(A), enforcement proceedings;
et al.

Documents re time guides or flat rate repair manuals used for repair of
automobiles. 2/25. Req. by: Robert LaRocca, Esq., of Kohn, Savett et al,
Philadelphia, Pa. Granted in part. 3/30. Exemptions: (b)(4), trade secrets;
(b)(7)(D), confidential source; et al.

Information re FTC investigation of possible antitrust violations of brokers'
multiple listing services, and trade associations in real estate industry. 2/18.
Req. by: Mr. Harry M. Snyder, Consumers Union of U.S., San Francisco, Calif.
Granted in part. 3/25. Exemptions: (b)(5), inter-intra agency memoranda;
(b)(7)(A), enforcement proceedings; et al.

FTC Compliance Manual for Fair Credit Reporting Act. 2/17. Req. by:
Sally J. Cummins, Esq., of Steptoe & Johnson, Washington, D.C. Granted. 2/20.

Information re Chrysler Corp's Warranty for Automobiles for Model Year 1978.
2/26. Req. by: William J. Schwarz, Jr., Esq., Bedford, N.Y. Granted. 3/12.

Market agreement executed between Pillsbury Co. and Kraft Inc. 2/23.
Req. by: Elroy H. Wolff, Esq., of Sidley & Austin, Washington, D.C. Denied.
3/23. Exemptions: (b)(3), specifically exempted by statute; (b)(4) trade secrets.

Documents re Norelco Black Pro rotary razor. 2/17. Req. by: David Barmak,
Esq., of Sherman, Fox et al, Washington, D.C. Denied. 3/19. Exemptions:
(b)(4), trade secrets; (b)(5), inter-intra agency memoranda; (b)(7)(A) enforcement
proceedings.

Material re vibration problems associated with 1979 Ford F-150 pick-up truck. 2/26. Req. by: Drew A. Hanna, Esq., of Hanna & Hanna, Bowling Green, Ohio. Granted in part. 3/17. Exemption: (b)(7)(D), confidential source.

Information re warranty offered by Quaker State Oil. 2/24. Req. by: Carl Shoolman, Esq., of Shoolman & Shoolman, Rochester, N.Y. Granted in part. 3/18. Exemptions: (b)(5), inter-intra agency memoranda; (b)(7)(D), confidential source.

Information re contract between FTC and Dr. Howard Marvel for analysis of vertical restraints in sale of hearing aids. 2/4. Req. by: Linda S. Peterson, of Sidley & Austin, Washington, D.C. Granted in part. 3/5. Exemptions: (b)(5), inter-intra agency memoranda; (b)(7)(A), enforcement proceedings.

Previously released information re Proctor & Gamble Co. backhaul allowance programs. 2/9. Req. by: Scott M. Chapin, Esq., of Convoy, Hewitt et al, New York, N.Y. Granted. 2/27.

Information re Annual Reports to Congress on Fair Debt Collection Practices Act. 2/10. Req. by: Michael J. Hungerford, Esq., Onondaga Neighborhood Legal Services, Syracuse, N.Y. Granted. 2/25.

Information re Outdoor Power Equip. Institute (OPEI) and Am. Nat'l Standards Institute, particularly in regard to issuance of safety standards for lawn mowers and lawn and garden tractors. 2/5. Req. by: Geoffrey N. Fieger, Esq., of Fieger, Cousens & Boesky, Southfield, Mich. Granted in part. 2/24. Exemption: (b)(5), inter-intra agency memoranda.

Previously released information re Appliance Energy Labeling Program for Water Heaters. 2/16. Req. by: Robert Bigelow, Computer Law Service, Woburn, Mass. Granted. 2/23.

Documents re release of premerger notification data to foreign governments under voluntary or bilateral agreements of co-operation in antitrust investigations. 2/4. Req. by: Mr. C. Douglas Welty, Univ. of Virginia School of Law, Charlottesville, Va. Granted in part. 2/23. Exemption: (b)(5), inter-intra agency memoranda.

Materials relating to three contracts which have been entered into by FTC's Div. of Marketing Abuses under Housing Condominium Programs. 2/2. Req. by: Kenneth G. Peters, Esq., of Colton & Boykin, Washington, D.C. Denied. 2/19. Exemptions: (b)(5), inter-intra agency memoranda; (b)(6), personnel records; (b)(7)(A), enforcement proceedings.

Documents re FTC investigation of Hoffman-LaRoche Inc., Nutley, N.J. 1/27. Req. by: James L. Rench, Esq., of Roetzel & Andress, Akron, Ohio. Denied. 2/12. Exemptions: (b)(4), trade secrets; (b)(7)(A), enforcement proceedings; et al.

Documents re FTC investigation of use of Chevette transmissions in mid-size and full-size GM automobiles. 1/19. Req. by: Haskel Bazell, Esq., Cincinnati, Ohio. Granted in part. 2/23. Exemptions: (b)(5), inter-intra agency memoranda; (b)(7)(A), enforcement proceedings; et al.

Reports and other documents examining fuel economy claims for gasoline additives. 1/20. Req. by: Robin L. Hirsch, Esq., of Hall, Dickler et al, New York, N.Y. Denied. 2/23. Exemptions: (b)(5), inter-intra agency memoranda; (b)(7)(A), enforcement proceedings; et al.

Access to all FOIA requests received since Jan. 1, 1976, re Phelps Dodge Industries, Inc. 1/20. Req. by: Michael E. Wiles, Esq., of Debevoise, Plimpton et al, New York, N.Y. Granted in part. 2/12. Exemptions: (b)(3), specifically exempted by statute; (b)(4), trade secrets; (b)(5), inter-intra agency memoranda.

Information re safety characteristics of AMC Jeep automobiles. 1/8. Req. by: Jim S. Adler, Esq., of Adler, Hazzard & Pettiette, Houston, Tex. Granted in part. 2/23. Exemptions: (b)(4), trade secrets; (b)(7)(A), enforcement proceedings.

Documents re practice of "transshipping" Levi Strauss clothing. 1/15. Req. by: Rodney E. Gould, Esq., of Rosenman, Colin et al, New York, N.Y. Granted in part. 2/20. Exemptions: (b)(5), inter-intra agency memoranda; (b)(7)(D), confidential source.

Investigative file re Suburban Collection Corp./Landlords Service Bureau. 1/12. Req. by: Mel Cahan, Esq., of Lurie & Cahan, Chicago, Ill. Granted in part. 2/12. Exemptions: (b)(5), inter-intra agency memoranda; (b)(7)(A), enforcement proceedings; et al.

Documents re Fedders Corp., particularly those relating to air conditioners, heat pumps, or split-system heat pumps. 1/2. Req. by: Peter J.P. Brickfield, Esq., of Patton, Boggs & Blow, Washington, D.C. Granted in part. 2/11. Exemptions: (b)(5), inter-intra agency memoranda; (b)(7)(A), enforcement proceedings; et al.

FTC Consent Order involving Beneficial Corp., File No. C-3032. 1/8. Req. by: LeRoy P. Shuster, Esq., Legal Services of Southeast Nebraska, Lincoln, Neb. Granted in part. 2/10. Exemptions: (b)(3), specifically exempted by statute; (b)(4), trade secrets.

Material re FTC investigation of Seiko Time Inc. 1/12. Req. by: Deborah M. Lodge, Esq., of Weil, Gotshal & Manges, New York, N.Y. Granted in part. 2/10. Exemptions: (b)(5), inter-intra agency memoranda; (b)(7)(D), confidential source; et al.

Consumer complaints re Chevrolet 454 Engine. 1/7. Req. by: James J. Kriva, Esq., of Denny & Yanisch, Milwaukee, Wisc. Granted in part. 2/9. Exemptions: (b)(7)(A), enforcement proceedings; (b)(7)(D), confidential source.

Records re divestiture of assets of Liquid Air Corp. 1/9. Req. by: Evelyn M. Suarez, Esq., of Bell, Boyd et al, Washington, D.C. Denied. 1/27. Exemptions: (b)(5), inter-intra agency memoranda; (b)(7)(A), enforcement proceedings.

Complaints and other data re alleged unfair or anticompetitive practices in catching, processing and sale of fish in the coastal waters between Seattle, Wash., and the Arctic Ocean. 1/5. Req. by: E. Charles Routh, Esq., of Garvey, Schubert et al, Seattle, Wash. Granted in part. 1/26. Exemptions: (b)(3), specifically exempted by statute; (b)(4), trade secrets; (b)(5), inter-intra agency memoranda.

Documents re investigation of alleged retail price maintenance by Rossignol Ski Co. 1/2. Req. by: Joseph M. Gensheimer, Esq., of Morgan, Lewis & Bockius, Washington, D.C. Denied. 1/21. Exemptions: (b)(7)(A), enforcement proceedings; (b)(5), inter-intra agency memoranda; et al.

Documents re defects in color or black and white television receivers. 12/15. Req. by: Kenneth S. Freedman, Esq., Chicago, Ill. Granted in part. 1/19. Exemption: (b)(7)(D), confidential source.

Information re K-Mart Enterprises Inc., particularly relating to requirement that scientific testing maintain a minimum confidence level before results may be used to justify product claims. 12/15. Req. by: Douglas J. Wood, Esq., of Hall, Dickler et al. Granted in part. 1/14. Exemptions: (b)(3), specifically exempted by statute; (b)(4), trade secrets.

Previously released information re alleged anticompetitive practices in beef industry and retail grocery industry. 12/22. Req. by: Roland W. Selman, Esq., of Pillsbury, Madison & Sutro, Washington, D.C. Granted in part. 1/13. Exemptions: (b)(5), inter-intra agency memoranda; (b)(7)(A), enforcement proceedings.

Complaints and other information re defects in 1977 model 530i BMW automobiles. 12/18. Req. by: Julius Rabinowitz, Esq., of Weil, Gothshal & Manges, New York, N.Y. Granted. 1/12.

Consumer complaints re engine problems in vehicles manufactured and/or distributed by Subaru of America Inc. and Fuji Heavy Industries Ltd. 12/15. Req. by: Law Offices of Michael R. Jencks, San Francisco, Calif. Granted in part. 1/7. Exemption: (b)(7)(D), confidential source.

Documents re cellular plastic foam insulation. 12/16. Req. by: Joel Schneider, Esq., of Frumkim & Manta, Philadelphia, Pa. Granted. 1/5.

## Food & Drug Administration
FOIA Office: (301) 443-6310

List of generic pharmaceutical manufacturers which are registered with FDA. 4/27. Req. by: E. Aymat, Attorney at Law.

Safety data re Injectible Silicon manufactured by Dow Corning. 4/27. Req. by: J. Krupnick, Esq., of Krupnick & Campbell.

Information re active ingredients for Dexatol manufactured by Neland Pharmaceuticals. 4/24. Req. by: A. Rosenbloom, Esq., of Dewey, Ballantine et al.

Information re "Essence of Strawberry Shampoo" distributed by K-Mart. 4/21. Req. by: M. Davich, Esq., of Keller & Katowsky.

EIR's and related documents for American Pacemaker Corp. 4/21. Req. by: J. Wilson, Esq., of Crosby, Heafey et al.

Safety data re: tetracycline medication called "Victrin," manufactured by Parke-Davis. 4/15. Req. by: J. Parton, Esq., of Lynch & Loofbourrow.

Information re Dewitt's Oil for Ear Use manufactured by Dewitt Int'l Corp. 4/15. Req. by: F. Gray, Esq., of Neiman, Neiman et al.

Consumer complaints re Thorotrast. 4/15. Req. by: M. Guth, Attorney at Law.

Information re Riviera Tanning Pills. 4/15. Req. by: J. Caparros, Attorney at Law.

FDA case histories re CU-7 intrauterine device. 4/15. Req. by: M. Chase, Esq., of Weinstein, Chayt & Bard.

Preliminary classification results for radiology devices. 4/13. Req. by: M. Oppenheimer, Esq., of Venable, Baetjer & Howard.

Information re baby food formula Neo-Mull-Soy manufactured by Syntex Corp. 4/13. Req. by: W. Pickett, Attorney at Law.

Complaint filed against Appian Way Cheese Pizza. 4/8. Req. by: A. O'Mara, Attorney at Law.

Safety information re drugs Delatutin and Provera. 4/7. Req. by: R. Solymosy, Esq., of Pegalis & Wachman.

Information re withdrawal of drug Nisentil. 4/7. Req. by: M. Larson, Esq., of Barbier, Goulet & Petersmar.

Any lot of oral polio vaccine by Lederle Labs between 1/1/80 and 1/1/81 found to be defective and recalled. 4/7. Req. by: W. Reis, Esq., of Warshafsky, Rotter et al.

Studies re potential future effects of Chloride Deficiency Formula. 4/2. Req. by: J. Connell, Esq., of Chooks, Low & Connell.

Adverse reactions and other information re "Betadine." 4/2. Req. by: J. Kusky, Esq., of Painin, Graber & Paul.

Information re toxic shock syndrome and Tampon-related complaints. 4/1. Req. by: R. Sauler, Esq., of Wald, Harkrader & Ross.

Adverse reaction reports re Desmopression Acetate manufactured by Ferring Pharmaceutical. 4/1. Req. by: P. Durso, Esq., of Fazzano & McGhail.

Information re "La Creme" manufactured by Kraft Inc. 3/31. Req. by: R. Schwartz, Esq., of Davis & Gilbert.

Adverse reactions re contraceptives with Nonoxynol-9.  3/25.  Req. by: E. Woocher, Esq., of Woocher & Woocher.

Certified copies of seven complaints filed against Heinz Baby Foods.  3/24. Req. by: T. Young, Esq., of Meyer, Tillberry & Body.

Safety data re following drugs: Provest by Upjohn; C-Quens by Eli Lilly; and Oracon by Mead Johnson.  3/23.  Req. by: H. Eisenberg, Esq., of Eisenberg & Yoffa.

Information re S-Pluss II Instrument, manufactured in connection with Hematology Reagents.  3/23.  Req. by: E.  Stoer, Esq., of Reed, Smith et al.

Computer printout of adverse reactions for "Fluothane." 3/18.  Req. by: R. Hall, Esq., of Hall, Surovell et al.

List of adverse reactions re "Metandren."  3/17.  Req. by: L. Ehrenberg, Esq., of Friedman & Shaftan.

Computer printout of adverse reactions re Haldol or Haloperidol.  3/16. Req. by: L. Karam, Attorney at Law.

Information re "Tofranil."  3/16.  Req. by: S. Lypinski, Attorney at Law.

Publication from Nat'l Library of Medicine re adverse effects of oral contraceptives 7/74 through 12/77.  3/16.  Req. by: R. Chin, Attorney at Law.

Safety information re Muller Type Total Hip Prosthesis.  3/16.  Req. by: P. Eisler, Attorney at Law.

FDA report re toxic shock syndrome and its relation to Rely tampons manufactured by Procter & Gamble.  3/16.  Req.  by: R. Goldstein, Esq., of Goldberg, Rubinstein & Buck.

Information re Medtronics Pacemaker, Model 5950.  3/16.  Req. by: S. Wright, Attorney at Law.

Data filed by Purdue Frederick Co. re Betadine Solution.  3/13.  Req. by: J. Kosky, Esq., of Pianin, Graber & Paull.

Information re: Hip Joint Prosthesis, Bechtol Femoral Component, manufactured by Richards Mfg. Co., Memphis, Tenn.  3/12.  Req. by: P. Fahr, Esq., of Carlsen, Greiner & Law.

Information re anti-miscarriage drug DES.  3/11.  Req. by: T. Foote, Esq., of Bourhis, Lawless & Harvey.

Test survey procedure form re: inspection dated 2/10/81 of microwave oven at Data Terminal Systems Inc., Maynard, Mass.  3/11.  Req. by: R. Harris, Attorney at Law.

List of New Drug Application (NDA) holders re Propoxphene Napsylate.  3/9. Req. by: R. Kingham, Esq., of Covington & Burling.

Adverse reactions re drug "Tetracycline." 3/9. Req. by: C. Collins, Esq., of Mead, Dore & Voute.

Information re anti-nausea drug Bendectin. 3/9. Req. by: R. Songer, Esq., of Law Offices of Thomas H. Bleakley.

Information re defective insulin manufactured by Eli Lilly & Co. 2/19. Req. by: R. Ward, Attorney a Law.

Filings since 1976 for following products: Oral Irrigation Device and Electric-Powered Toothbrush. 2/18. Req. by: E. Karas, Esq., of Arnold & Porter.

Complaints re: Dentifrice and Dental Care. 2/18. Req. by: S. Lapine, Esq., of Keller & Heckman.

Information re "Atromid-S." 2/18. Req. by: J. Rogers, Esq., of McDonough, Beyer et al.

Material re "Arosurf" manufactured by Ashland Chemical Co., Dublin, Ohio. 2/18. Req. by: A. Wisti, Esq., of Wisti & Jaaskelainen.

Information re drug "Dynapen." 2/11. Req. by: J. Brophy, Attorney at Law.

Minutes re 1980 session of Fertility & Maternal Health Drug Advisory Committee. 2/10. Req. by: M. Austrian, Esq., of Collier, Shannon et al.

Information re sale of frozen yogurt products. 2/10. Req. by: K. Logwood, Esq., of Stroock, Stroock & Lavan.

Consumer complaints re Sauna Slim Shorts manufactured by Rush Inc. 2/10. Req. by: H. Shackle, Attorney at Law.

Information re Noxema Medicated Shave Cream. 2/10. Req. by: S. Wade, Esq., of Fales & Fales.

Information re injuries associated with use of wheelchairs. 2/9. Req. by: B. Fieger, Esq., of Fieger, Cousens & Boesky.

Safety data re: issuance of approval letter concerning "Ibuprofen," manufactured by Boots Pharmaceuticals Inc. 2/9. Req. by: S. Temko, Esq., of Covington & Burling.

Information re drug "Tagamet." 2/9. Req. by: H. Watstein, Esq., of Watstein & Watstein.

FDA investigative file re use of "Orthene" on various tomato crops. 2/9. Req. by: R. Artiano, Esq., of Stutz, McCormick et al.

Adverse reactions re Intraocular Lens Implants, Model 017, manufactured by Intermedics Inc. 2/5. Req. by: M. Simon, Esq., of Weaver & Willman.

Complaints re Insta-Perm manufactured by Lamaur Inc. 2/5. Req. by: L. Force, Esq., of Force & Baldwin.

Recall information re Dalkon Shield intrauterine device. 2/3. Req. by: C. Lieberman, Esq., of Machles & Liberman.

Information re recall of "Training Fork & Spoonset" imported by Cribmates Inc. 2/2. Req. by: S. Scherr, Esq., Natural Resources Defense Council.

Information re product experience with vibrator belts. 1/26. Req. by: W. Hudman, Esq., of Cuba, Simmon & Hudman.

Consumer complaints re IUD Lippes Loop. 1/26. Req. by: B. Overmann, Esq., of Beckman, Lavercombe et al.

Information re investigation of drug Lincocin manufactured by Upjohn Co. 1/26. Req. by: S. Van Camp, Esq., of Miller, Pitt & Feldman.

Documents re Betamethosone and Vasodilan. 1/26. Req. by: T. Schrag, Esq., of Storm, Schrag et al.

Information re Multi-Hormone treatment. 1/23. Req. by: H. Rothblatt, Esq., of Rothblatt, Rothblatt & Seijas.

FDA studies re synthetic human growth hormone and Genentech Inc. 1/23. Req. by: E. Allera, Esq., of Perito, Duerk et al.

Information re drug Baralgine manufactured by Hoechst Labs. 1/23. Req. by: R. Sokol, Attorney at Law.

EIR's for Professional Contact Lens Co., Orlando, Fla. 1/21. Req. by: M. Shapiro, Esq., of Kleinfeld, Kaplan et al.

Information re Norelco Black Pro Rotary Razor manufactured by North American Phillips Corp. 1/21. Req. by: D. Barmak, Esq., of Sherman, Fox et al.

## Department of Labor
FOIA Office: (202) 523-6438

Copy of Wage & Hour investigative files re Torrance Memorial Hosp. Medical Center. Req. by: Gerald Goldman, Esq., Los Angeles, Calif. Denied. 3/10. Exemption: (b)(7)(A), enforcement proceedings.

Fair Labor Standards investigative file for Computel Systems Inc., Miami, Fla. Req. by: Mark S. Berman, Esq., of Bryson & Berman, Miami, Fla. Granted in part. 3/10. Exemption: (b)(7)(D), confidential source.

Labor Management Services Adm. (LMSA) investigative files for San Joaquin Administrators. Req. by: Gerson F. Goldsmith, Esq., of Goldsmith, Siegel et al, Portland, Ore. Denied. 3/10. Exemption: (b)(7)(A), enforcement proceedings.

Wage & Hour investigative files for Travel Funtastic Inc. Req. by: Les Weisbrod, Esq., Dallas, Tex. Denied. 3/10. Exemption: (b)(7)(A), enforcement proceedings.

Copy of OSHA investigative file re accident at Harbor Dev. Co. Gulfport, Miss. Req. by: Norman Breland, Esq., of Breland & Barnett, Gulfport, Miss. Granted in part. 1/19. Exemptions: (b)(5), inter-intra agency memoranda; (b)(7)(C), invasion of personal privacy; (b)(7)(D), confidential source.

OSHA investigative file re Nat'l Underground Constr. Co. Req. by: Joseph A. Camarra, Esq., of Cassiday, Schade & Gloor, Chicago, Ill. Denied. 1/16. Exemption: (b)(7)(A), enforcement proceedings.

OSHA investigative file re accidental death of employee at Bethlehem Steel Corp., Bethlehem, Pa. Req. by: Arnold J. Falk, Esq., Easton, Pa. Granted in part. 1/9. Exemptions: (b)(7)(C), invasion of personal privacy; (b)(7)(D), confidential source.

Investigative file re Maloof's Dep't Store, Atlanta, Ga. Req. by: Bruce Beerman, Esq., of Smith, Cohen et al, Atlanta, Ga. Granted in part. 1/9. Exemption: (b)(7)(D), confidential source.

Copy of investigative files of Federal Contract Compliance Programs re alleged employment discrimination practices against Hispanics by Univ. of Colorado Medical Center. Req. by: Remigio Pete Reyes, Esq., Denver, Colo. Denied. 1/7. Exemption: (b)(7)(A), enforcement proceedings.

Wage & Hour Div. investigative file re age discrimination complaint against Getty Oil Co., Houston, Tex. Req. by: Dennis C. Colby, Esq., of Lohmann, Glazer & Irwin, Houston, Tex. Granted in part. 1/7. Exemptions: (b)(7)(C), invasion of personal privacy; (b)(7)(D), confidential source.

Investigative files of Office of Federal Contract Compliance Programs re Nat'l City Bank, Cleveland, Ohio. Req. by: Darryl E. Pittman, Esq., of Mosely, Goodman & Pittman, Cleveland, Ohio. Denied. 1/7. Exemption: (b)(7)(A), enforcement proceedings.

Copy of Pension & Welfare Benefits Program investigative file re employee benefit programs operated by Teamsters Local #959 (Alaska). Req. by: C. Floyd Matthews, Esq., of Birch, Horton et al, Washington, D.C. Denied. 1/7. Exemption: (b)(7)(A), enforcement proceedings.

Information re DOL's certification of workers of Brierwood Shoe Corp., Kutztown, Penn., for trade adjustment assistance. Req. by: Gregory P.N. Joseph, Esq., of Fried, Frank et al, New York, N.Y. Granted in part. 1/6. Exemption: (b)(4), trade secrets.

## National Labor Relations Board
FOIA Office: (202) 254-9350

Copies of advice memoranda re "Endicott College," Case #1-CA-12,171, and "St. John's Univ., New York," Case #29-CB-1858. Req. by: Ms. Gretchen Haase, of Oppenheimer Law Firm, St. Paul, Minn. Granted. 3/25.

Advice memorandum re "Grand Bassa Tankers Inc.," Case #29-CA-8153 and 8215; 29-CC-727 and 728. Req. by: Jos. Dinsmore Murphy, Esq., of Smiley, Murphy et al, Washington, D.C. Granted. 3/18.

Memorandum dated July 31, 1980, from General Counsel re "American Farm Lines." Case #16-CA-9103. Req. by: Sue Ratchford, of Bryon, Cave et al, St. Louis, Mo. Granted. 3/3.

Letter from Mr. Telanoff of NLRB Office of Appeals (Nov. 26, 1980) re "California Teachers Assoc.," Case #21-CA-18420. Req. by: Michael J. Feinberg, Esq., of Schwartz, Steinsapir et al, Los Angeles, Calif. Granted. 3/2.

NLRB report re elections won and lost by Retail Clerks Int'l Union and Hotel & Restaurant Employees Union from Jan. 1, 1978, to present. Req. by: Thomas J. Higgins, Esq., of Stoneman, Chandler & Miller, Boston, Mass. Granted. 3/2.

Information re United Food & Commercial Workers Int'l Union, AFL-CIO, Case #13-CA-20371. Req. by: Marshall J. Bailey, Esq., of Streamwood, Ill. Granted in part. 2/12. Exemption: (b)(5), inter-intra agency memoranda.

Data re NLRB and court proceedings concerning bargaining orders in lieu of an election. Req. by: Jerrold Mehlman, Esq., Asst. General Counsel, J.P. Stevens & Co., New York, N.Y. Granted. 2/6.

Copy of appeal in "Craft-Maid Inc.," Case #4-CA-11043. Req. by: Richard S. Boris, Esq., of Moss & Boris, New York, N.Y. Granted. 2/4.

**Nuclear Regulatory Commission**
FOIA Office: (301) 492-7211

Information re plutonium unaccounted for by Nuclear Fuel Services of Ervin, Tex. Req. by: John Vail, Esq., Legal Services of Upper East Tennessee Inc., Johnson City, Tenn. Granted. 12/24.

Records re potential environmental impact associated with fuel loading and/or low power testing of Diablo Canyon Nuclear Power Plant. Req. by: Herbert H. Brown, Esq., of Hill, Christopher & Phillips, Washington, D.C. Granted. 12/22.

Copy of damage claim filed against NRC by General Public Utilities Corp. on Dec. 8, 1980. Req. by: John W. Pestle, Esq., of Varnum, Riddering et al, Grand Rapids, Mich. Granted. 12/16.

Information re fire protection requirements as contained in 10 CFR Part 50, Appendix R. Req. by: McNeill Watkins, II, Esq., of Debevoise & Liberman, Washington, D.C. Granted. 12/9.

Copy of September 1980 report by Office of Analysis & Evaluation of Operational Data (AEOD) re interim equipment and procedures at Brown's Ferry to detect water in discharge volume. Req. by: Ellyn R. Weiss, Esq., of Harmon & Weiss. Granted. 10/31.

**Office of the Comptroller of the Currency**
FOIA Office: (202) 447-0025

Letters from Richard Fitzgerald, OCC, to Chrysler Credit Corp. re applicability of bonding limits. Req. by: Sheryl R. Romeo, of Mayer, Brown & Platt, Washington, D.C. Granted in part. 3/12. Exemptions: (b)(4), trade secrets; (b)(6), personnel records.

Copies of feasibility studies re Women's Nat'l Bank and Diplomat Nat'l Bank, both of Washington, D.C. Req. by: Helen Kanorsky, of Dickstein, Shapiro & Morin, Washington, D.C. Granted. 3/10.

Information re recent tender offer by Crown Bancshares for stock in Mercantile Nat'l Bank, Topeka, Kans. Req. by: William L. Small, Esq., Nashville, Tenn. Granted. 3/5.

Copy of tender offer filed by J. Albritton 2/9/80 to purchase shares of Riggs Nat'l Bank, Washington, D.C. Req. by: William A. Englehart, Esq., of Chapman & Paul, Washington, D.C. Granted. 3/5.

OCC letter dated 6/27/78 to 1st City Nat'l Bank, Houston, Tex., re loaning securities on behalf of agency account. Req. by: Ellen Bickal, Esq., of Emmet, Marvin & Marton, New York, N.Y. Granted. 2/23.

Certified by-laws and articles of incorporation re Riggs Nat'l Bank, Washington, D.C. Req. by: Ms. Paul Poulos, of Fulbright & Jaworski, Washington, D.C. Granted. 2/19.

Documents re acquisition of Fidelity Nat'l Bank, California. Req. by: M. Ann Spudis, of Sullivan & Cromwell, New York, N.Y. Granted. 2/5.

Records re merger involving Bank of Nevada. Req. by: W. Bruce Beckley, Esq., of Beckley, Singleton et al, Las Vegas, Nev. Granted. 1/14.

Interpretations re graduated mortgages, especially concerning 12 USC 371(A)(1) -- 30 year amortizations. Req. by: T. Eugene Allen, III, Esq., of Nexsen, Pruet et al, Columbia, S.C. Granted in part. 12/15. Exemptions: (b)(4), trade secrets; (b)(6), personnel records.

Documents from file of Nat'l Bank (N.B.) San Francisco. Req. by: Warren F. Chapman, Esq., of Lee & Li, San Francisco, Calif. Granted in part. 12/11/80. Exemptions: (b)(4), trade secrets; (b)(6), personnel records.

Agreements and decisions re three mergers: (1) Pacific N.B. of Washington/ American Commonwealth Bank, Spokane, Wash.; (2) Peoples N.B. of Washington/Columbia Bank, Wash.; (3) FNB of New Jersey/Commonwealth N.B., Metuchen, N.J. Req. by: Frank Zaffere, Esq., of Reuben & Proctor, Chicago, Ill. Granted. 12/10/80.

**Securities & Exchange Commission**
FOIA Office: (202) 523-5530

Information re Am. Bakeries Co. et al. Req. by: John D. Seiver, Esq., of Cole, Raywid & Braverman, Washington, D.C. Granted. 5/1.

Material re "illegal payment" investigation of Columbia Pictures.  3/31.
Req. by:  Richard M. Meyer, Esq., of Milberg, Weiss et al, New York, N.Y.
Granted.  4/21.

Previously released information re MacMillan Ring-Free Oil Co.  3/31.
Req. by: Paul G. Thomas, Esq., of Collier, Shannon et al, Washington, D.C.
Granted.  4/21.

Documents re SEC investigations of Catawba Corp.  3/31.  Req. by: Mr. Larry
Ottinger, Foundation for Nat'l Progress, San Francisco, Calif.  Denied.  4/20.
Exemption: (b)(7)(A), enforcement proceedings.

Information re Chicago Board Options Exchange.  3/23.  Req. by: Mahlon M.
Frankhauser, Esq., of Kirkland & Ellis, Washington, D.C.  Granted in part.  4/20.
Exemptions: (b)(5), inter-intra agency memoranda; (b)(7)(C), invasion of personal
privacy.

SEC investigative file re Litton Systems Inc.  3/26.  Req. by: Josephine L.
Urisini, Esq., of Fried, Frank et al, Washington, D.C.  Denied.  4/20.
Exemption: (b)(7)(A), enforcement proceedings.

Documents re SEC's investigation of Commonwealth Western Corp.  4/17.
Req. by: Robert D. Levy, Esq., of Conway & Levy, Albuquerque, N.M.  Denied.
4/17.  Exemption: (b)(7)(A), enforcement proceedings.

Material re Control Data Corp.  4/6.  Req. by: Mr. Stanley Crock, Wall
Street Journal, Washington, D.C.  Denied.  4/23.  Exemption: (b)(7)(A),
enforcement proceedings.

SEC investigation file re O.P.M. Leasing Services Inc.  3/17.  Req. by:
Patricia L. Truscelli, Esq., of Parker, Chapin et al, New York, N.Y.  Denied.
4/23.  Exemption: (b)(7)(A), enforcement proceedings.

Information re CMT Investment Trust.  4/3.  Req. by: Martin A. Bell, Esq.,
of Finley, Kumble et al, New York, N.Y.  Granted in part.  4/22.  Exemptions:
(b)(5), inter-intra agency memoranda; (b)(7)(C), invasion of personal privacy.

Records re Investors Equity Inc. et al.  4/3.  Req. by: Gerald J. Newbrough,
Esq., of Nyemaster, Goode et al, Des Moines, Iowa.  Granted in part.  4/21.
Exemption: (b)(5), inter-intra agency memoranda.

Material re Pennsylvania Life Co.  3/16.  Req. by: Robert J. Grossman,
Esq., of Hecht, Diamond & Greenfield, Pacific Palisades, Calif.  Granted in
part.  4/22.  Exemptions: (b)(4), trade secrets; (b)(5), inter-intra agency
memoranda; (b)(7)(C), invasion of personal privacy.

Information re SEC investigation of General Arizona Clearing House Corp. et
al.  3/24.  Req. by: Owen C. Rouse, Esq., of Ireland, Stapleton & Pryor,
Denver, Colo.  Denied.  4/17.  Exemption: (b)(7)(A), enforcement proceedings.

Documents re Starr Broadcasting Group, Inc.  Req. by: Stephen T. Rodd,
Esq., New York, N.Y.  Granted in part.  4/16.  Exemptions: (b)(4), trade secrets;
(b)(5) inter-intra agency memoranda; (b)(7)(C), invasion of personal privacy.

Proxy statements dated 3/26/80 and 2/13/81 as filed by Cash Reserve Management Inc. 3/27. Req. by: Richard B. Dannenberg, Esq., of Lowey, Dannenberg & Knapp, New York, N.Y. Granted. 4/14.

SEC investigative file on Foster & Marshall Inc. (S-1532). Req. by: Mr. Mark Bender, of Paine, Lowe et al, Spokane, Wash. Granted in part. 4/14. Exemptions: (b)(4), trade secrets; (b)(5), inter-intra agency memoranda; (b)(7)(C), invasion of personal privacy.

Investigative file on Olympia Brewing Co. stock, Loeb Rhoades and its agent R. Jack Bernhardt. 3/12. Req. by: John T. Doyle, Esq., of Joyce & Kubasiak, Chicago, Ill. Denied. 4/13. Exemption: (b)(7)(A), enforcement proceedings.

Previously released information re AES Technology Sys. Inc. 3/23. Req. by: Stuart D. Wechsler, Esq., of Kass, Goodkind et al, New York, N.Y. Granted. 4/10.

Information re acquisition by Grumman Corp. of the Flexible Co. 3/23. Req. by: Judah I. Labovitz, Esq., of Pomerantz, Levy et al, New York, N.Y. Granted. 4/10.

Records re Am. General Corp. and its subsidiaries. 1/20. Req. by: Robert C. Sheehan, Esq., of Skadden, Arps et al, New York, N.Y. Granted in part. 4/10. Exemptions: (b)(5), inter-intra agency memoranda; (b)(7)(C), invasion of personal privacy.

Documents re Seagram Corp. Ltd. et al. 3/18. Req. by: Barry A. Weprin, Esq., of Wachtell, Lipton et al, New York, N.Y. Granted. 4/8.

Information re SEC investigation of Litton Industries Inc. 3/13. Req. by: Harvey Kurzweil, Esq., of Dewey, Ballantine et al, Washington, D.C. Denied. 4/7. Exemption: (b)(7)(A), enforcement proceedings.

Documents re SEC investigative file in matter of Gov't Securities Management Co. 3/9. Req. by: Peter M. Saparoof, Esq., of Gaston Snow et al, Boston, Mass. Granted in part. 3/27. Exemption: (b)(5), inter-intra agency memoranda.

SEC investigative file of Foster & Marshall Inc. (S-1532). 3/3. Req. by: Mr. Mark Bender, of Paine, Lowe et al, Spokane, Wash. Granted in part. 3/26. Exemptions: (b)(5), inter-intra agency memoranda; (b)(7)(C), invasion of personal privacy.

Copy of FOIA request letter re Am. Birthright Trust. 3/18. Req. by: Allan S. Mostoff, Esq., of Dechert Price & Rhoads, Washington, D.C. Granted. 3/26.

Investigation file re First Arabian Corp. 3/9. Req. by: Richard D. Haynes, Esq., of Haynes & Boone, Dallas, Tex. Denied. 3/26. Exemption: (b)(7)(A), enforcement proceedings.

Material re Olympic Gas & Oil Co. 3/12. Req. by: Mr. James Cunningham, of Cunningham & Burnette, Washington, D.C. Denied. 3/26. Exemption: (b)(7)(A), enforcement proceedings.

Information re Florida Power Corp. Req. by: John B. Williams, Esq., of Collier, Shannon et al, Washington, D.C. Granted. 3/17.

Records re Gran-Park Securities Inc. et al. 2/25. Req. by: Linda H. Nelson, Esq., of Landfield, Becker & Green, Washington, D.C. Denied. 3/12. Exemption: (b)(7)(A), enforcement proceedings.

Material re Chicago Bd. Options Exchange proposal to trade GNMA options. 2/25. Req. by: Anne M. Gallagher, Esq., of Kirkland & Ellis, Washington, D.C. Granted in part. 3/11. Exemptions: (b)(4), trade secrets; (b)(5), inter-intra agency memoranda; et al.

SEC investigative file re Esmark Inc. 2/24. Req. by: Arthur T. Susman, Esq., of Prins, Flamm & Susman, Chicago, Ill. Denied. 3/10. Exemption: (b)(7)(A), enforcement proceedings.

Information re SEC investigation of Hawaii Corp. 2/12. Req. by: W. Sidney Davis, Esq., of Davis, Market et al, New York, N.Y. Granted in part. 3/6. Exemption: (b)(7)(A), enforcement proceedings.

Documents re Vernitron Corp. 2/9. Req. by: Edward T. Dangel, III, Esq., of Dangel & Sherry, Boston, Mass. Granted in part. 3/6. Exemptions: (b)(4), trade secrets; (b)(5), inter-intra agency memoranda; (b)(7)(C), invasion of personal privacy.

Documents re previous request to inspect money market fund files located in SEC regional offices. 1/28. Req. by: John A. Dudley, Esq., of Sullivan & Worcester, Washington, D.C. Denied. 2/13. Exemptions: (b)(4), trade secrets; (b)(5), inter-intra agency memoranda.

SEC investigation file re OKC Corp. et al. 1/20. Req. by: I. Walton Bader, Esq., of Bader & Bader, White Plains, N.Y. Denied. 2/12. Exemption: (b)(7)(A), enforcement proceedings; et al.

Transcripts of testimony for Thomas J. O'Donnell and Louis Bravmann, taken in connection with investigation of Oppenheimer & Co. 1/21. Req. by: John L. Evans, Jr., Esq., of Graydon, Head & Ritchey, Cincinnati, Ohio. Granted in part. 2/12. Exemption: (b)(7)(C), invasion of personal privacy.

Documents re SEC investigation of Beneficial Standard Corp. et al. 1/13. Req. by: Bertrand M. Cooper, Esq., of O'Melveny & Myers, Los Angeles, Calif. Denied. 2/12. Exemption: (b)(7)(A), enforcement proceedings.

SEC investigation file re: Catawba Corp., Coastal Caribbean Oils & Minerals Ltd., and Richard C. Mayberry. 1/22. Req. by: Kenneth E. Krosin, Esq., of Howrey & Simon, Washington, D.C.

Information re Merrill Lynch's Cash Management Account Program & CMA Money Trust.  1/27.  Req. by: Mr. Ken Lieberman, Deposit & Credit Systems, San Francisco, Calif.  Granted in part.  3/25.  Exemptions: (b)(4), trade secrets; (b)(5), inter-intra agency memoranda.

SEC investigation file in matter of Phoenix Energy Co. et al.  12/29. Req. by: Eugene W. Landy, Esq., Landy & Spector, Eatontown, N.J.  Denied.  3/25. Exemption: (b)(7)(A), enforcement proceedings.

Investigation file re Devonshire Inc. et al.  3/3.  Req. by: Raymond King, Esq., of Buchalter, Nemer et al, Los Angeles, Calif.  Denied.  3/25.  Exemption: (b)(7)(A), enforcement proceedings.

Document re Boeing Corp.  3/3.  Req. by: Geoffrey H.  Ward, Esq., of Satterlee & Stephens, New York, N.Y.  Denied.  3/24.  Exemption: (b)(7)(A), enforcement proceedings.

Investigation file re Citizens & Southern Realty Investors (HO-1056). Req. by: Cyrus J. Gardner, Esq., of Barash & Hill, Los Angeles, Calif.  Granted in part.  3/24.  Exemptions: (b)(4), trade secrets; (b)(5), inter-intra agency memoranda; et al.

Documents re Int'l Systems & Controls Corp. (HO-1014).  Req. by: Stephen K. Halpert, Esq., of Skadden, Arps et al, Boston, Mass.  Granted in part. 3/23.  Exemptions: (b)(5), inter-intra agency memoranda; (b)(7)(C), invasion of personal privacy.

Previously released information re SEC investigation of Firestone Tire & Rubber Co.  3/9.  Req. by: Anne M. Gallagher, Esq., of Kirkland & Ellis, Washington, D.C.  Granted.  3/20.

Information re SEC policy with regard to enforcement of "illegal payments" allegations.  12/3.  Req. by: John M. Dowd, Esq., of Whitman & Ransom, Washington, D.C.  Granted.  3/20.

Documents re Investors Equity Inc. et al.  3/2.  Req. by: Gerald J. Newbrough, Esq., of Nyemaster, Goode et al, Des Moines, Iowa.  Granted.  3/18.

Material re SEC investigation of Sagittarius Fund Inc.  (NY-5064). Req. by: Nancy B. Turck, Esq., of Shearman & Sterling, New York, N.Y.  Granted in part.  3/18.  Exemptions: (b)(5), inter-intra agency memoranda; (b)(7)(C), invasion of personal privacy.

Information re SEC's investigation of government related securities as summarized in report published by Treasury-SECFed. Reserve Bd in Dec. 1980. 1/30.  Req. by: Roger McDaniel, Esq., of Cleary, Gottlieb et al, New York, N.Y.  Granted in part.  3/18.  Exemptions: (b)(7)(A), enforcement proceedings; (b)(7)(C), invasion of personal privacy.

SEC investigative files of Price Co. (HO-795) and Vernitron Corp. (HO-1035). 3/3.  Req. by: Raymond King, Esq., of Buchalter, Nemer et al, Los Angeles, Calif.  Granted in part.  3/17.  Exemptions: (b)(4), trade secrets; (b)(5), inter-intra agency memoranda; et al.

# APPENDIX A

## FREEDOM OF INFORMATION ACT

FREEDOM OF INFORMATION ACT

### § 552. Public information; agency rules, opinions, orders, records, and proceedings.

(a) Each agency shall make available to the public information as follows:

(1) Each agency shall separately state and currently publish in the Federal Register for the guidance of the public—

(A) descriptions of its central and field organization and the established places at which, the employees (and in the case of a uniformed service, the members) from whom, and the methods whereby, the public may obtain information, make submittals or requests, or obtain decisions;

(B) statements of the general course and method by which its functions are channeled and determined, including the nature and requirements of all formal and informal procedures available;

(C) rules of procedure, descriptions of forms available or the places at which forms may be obtained, and instructions as to the scope and contents of all papers, reports, or examinations;

(D) substantive rules of general applicability adopted as authorized by law, and statements of general policy or interpretations of general applicability formulated and adopted by the agency; and

(E) each amendment, revision, or repeal of the foregoing.

Except to the extent that a person has actual and timely notice of the terms thereof, a person may not in any manner be required to resort to, or be adversely affected by, a matter required to be published in the Federal Register and not so published. For the purpose of this paragraph, matter reasonably available to the class of persons affected thereby is deemed published in the Federal Register when incorporated by reference therein with the approval of the Director of the Federal Register.

(2) Each agency, in accordance with published rules, shall make available for public inspection and copying—

(A) final opinions, including concurring and dissenting opinions, as well as orders, made in the adjudication of cases;

(B) those statements of policy and interpretations which have been adopted by the agency and are not published in the Federal Register; and

(C) administrative staff manuals and instructions to staff that affect a member of the public;

unless the materials are promptly published and copies offered for sale. To the extent required to prevent a clearly unwarranted invasion of personal privacy, an agency may delete identifying details when it makes available or publishes an opinion, statement of policy, interpretation, or staff manual or instruction. However, in each case the justification for the deletion shall be explained fully in writing. Each agency shall also maintain and make available for public inspection and copying current indexes providing identifying information for the public as to any matter issued, adopted, or promulgated after July 4, 1967, and required by this paragraph to be made available or published. Each agency shall promptly publish, quarterly or more frequently, and distribute (by sale or otherwise) copies of each index or supplements thereto unless it determines by order published in the Federal Register that the publication would be unnecessary and impracticable, in which case the agency shall nonetheless provide copies of such index on request at a cost not to exceed the direct cost of duplication. A final order, opinion, statement of policy, interpretation, or staff manual or instruction that affects a member of the public may be relied on, used, or cited as precedent by an agency against a party other than an agency only if—

    (i) it has been indexed and either made available or published as provided by this paragraph; or

    (ii) the party has actual and timely notice of the terms thereof.

(3) Except with respect to the records made available under paragraphs (1) and (2) of this subsection, each agency, upon any request for records which (A) reasonably describes such records and (B) is made in accordance with published rules stating the time, place, fees (if any), and procedures to be followed, shall make the records promptly available to any person.

(4)(A) In order to carry out the provisions of this section, each agency shall promulgate regulations, pursuant to notice and receipt of public comment, specifying a uniform schedule of fees applicable to all constituent units of such agency. Such fees shall be limited to reasonable standard charges for document search and duplication and provide for recovery of only the direct costs of such search and duplication. Documents shall be furnished without charge or at a reduced charge where the agency determines that waiver or reduction of the fee is in the public interest because furnishing the information can be considered as primarily benefiting the general public.

(B) On complaint, the district court of the United States in the district in which the complainant resides, or has his principal place of business, or in which the agency records are situated, or in the District of Columbia, has jurisdiction to enjoin the agency from withholding agency records and to order the production of any agency records improperly withheld from the complainant. In such a case the court shall determine the matter de novo, and may examine the contents of such agency records in camera to determine whether such records or any part thereof shall be withheld under any of the exemptions set forth in subsection (b) of this section, and the burden is on the agency to sustain its action.

(C) Notwithstanding any other provisions of law, the defendant shall serve an answer or otherwise plead to any complaint made under this subsection within thirty days after service upon the defendant of the pleading in which such complaint is made, unless the court otherwise directs for good cause shown.

(D) Except as to cases the court considers of greater importance, proceedings before the district court, as authorized by this subsection, and appeals therefrom, take precedence on the docket over all cases and shall be assigned for hearing and trial or for argument at the earliest practicable date and expedited in every way.

(E) The court may assess against the United States reasonable attorney fees and other litigation costs reasonably incurred in any case under this section in which the complainant has substantially prevailed.

(F) Whenever the court orders the production of any agency records improperly withheld from the complainant and assesses against the United States reasonable attorney fees and other litigation costs, and the court additionally issues a written finding that the circumstances surrounding the withholding raise questions whether agency personnel acted arbitrarily or capriciously with respect to the withholding, the Civil Service Commission shall promptly initiate a proceeding to determine whether disciplinary action is warranted against the officer or employee who was primarily responsible for the withholding. The Commission, after investigation and consideration of the evidence submitted, shall submit its findings and recommendations to the administrative authority of the agency concerned and shall send copies of the findings and recommendations to the officer or employee or his representative. The administrative authority shall take the corrective action that the Commission recommends.

(G) In the event of noncompliance with the order of the court, the district court may punish for contempt the responsible employee, and in the case of a uniformed service, the responsible member.

(5) Each agency having more than one member shall maintain and make available for public inspection a record of the final votes of each member in every agency proceeding.

(6)(A) Each agency, upon any request for records made under paragraph (1), (2), or (3) of this subsection, shall—

(i) determine within ten days (excepting Saturdays, Sundays, and legal public holidays) after the receipt of any such request whether to comply with such request and shall immediately notify the person making such request of such determination and the reasons therefor, and of the right of such person to appeal to the head of the agency any adverse determination; and

(ii) make a determination with respect to any appeal within twenty days (excepting Saturdays, Sundays, and legal public holidays) after the receipt of such appeal. If on appeal the denial of the request for records is in whole or in part upheld, the agency shall notify the person making such request of the provisions for judicial review of that determination under paragraph (4) of this subsection.

(B) In unusual circumstances as specified in this subparagraph, the time limits prescribed in either clause (i) or clause (ii) of subparagraph (A) may be extended by written notice to the person making such request setting forth the reasons for such extension and the date on which a determination is expected to be dispatched. No such notice shall specify a date that would result in an extension for more than ten working days. As used in this subparagraph, "unusual circumstances" means, but only to the extent reasonably necessary to the proper processing of the particular request—

(i) the need to search for and collect the requested records from field facilities or other establishments that are separate from the office processing the request;

(ii) the need to search for, collect, and appropriately examine a voluminous amount of separate and distinct records which are demanded in a single request; or

(iii) the need for consultation, which shall be conducted with all practicable speed, with another agency having a substantial interest in the determination of the request or among two or more components of the agency having substantial subject-matter interest therein.

(C) Any person making a request to any agency for records under paragraph (1), (2), or (3) of this subsection shall be deemed to have exhausted his administrative remedies with respect to such request if the agency fails to comply with the application time limit provisions of this paragraph. If the Government can show exceptional circumstances exist and that the agency is exercising due diligence in responding to the request, the court may retain jurisdiction and allow the agency additional time to complete its review of the records. Upon any determination by an agency to comply with a request for records, the records shall be made promptly available to such person making such request. Any notification of denial of any request for records under this subsection shall set forth the names and titles or positions of each person responsible for the denial of such request.

(b) This section does not apply to matters that are—

(1)(A) specifically authorized under criteria established by an Executive order to be kept secret in the interest of national defense or foreign policy and (B) are in fact properly classified pursuant to such Executive order;

(2) related solely to the internal personnel rules and practices of an agency;

(3) specifically exempted from disclosure by statute (other than section 552b of this title), provided that such statute (A) requires that the matters be withheld from the public in such a manner as to leave no discretion on the issue, or (B) establishes particular criteria for withholding or refers to particular types of matters to be withheld;

(4) trade secrets and commercial or financial information obtained from a person and privileged or confidential;

(5) inter-agency or intra-agency memorandums or letters which would not be available by law to a party other than an agency in litigation with the agency;

(6) personnel and medical files and similar files the disclosure of which would constitute a clearly unwarranted invasion of personal privacy;

(7) investigatory records compiled for law enforcement purposes, but only to the extent that the production of such records would (A) interfere with enforcement proceedings, (B) deprive a person of a right to a fair trial or an impartial adjudication, (C) constitute an unwarranted invasion of personal privacy, (D) disclose the identity of a confidential source and, in the case of a record compiled by a criminal law enforcement authority in the course of a criminal investigation, or by an agency conducting a lawful national security intelligence investigation, confidential information furnished only by the confidential source, (E) disclose investigative techniques and procedures, or (F) endanger the life or physical safety of law enforcement personnel;

(8) contained in or related to examination, operating, or condition reports prepared by, on behalf of, or for the use of an agency

responsible for the regulation or supervision of financial institutions; or

(9) geological and geophysical information and data, including maps, concerning wells.

Any reasonably segregable portion of a record shall be provided to any person requesting such record after deletion of the portions which are exempt under this subsection.

(c) This section does not authorize withholding of information or limit the availability of records to the public, except as specifically stated in this section. This section is not authority to withhold information from Congress.

(d) On or before March 1 of each calendar year, each agency shall submit a report covering the preceding calendar year to the Speaker of the House of Representatives and President of the Senate for referral to the appropriate committees of the Congress. The report shall include—

(1) the number of determinations made by such agency not to comply with requests for records made to such agency under subsection (a) and the reasons for each such determination;

(2) the number of appeals made by persons under subsection (a)(6), the result of such appeals, and the reason for the action upon each appeal that results in a denial of information;

(3) the names and titles or positions of each person responsible for the denial of records requested under this section, and the number of instances of participation for each;

(4) the results of each proceeding conducted pursuant to subsection (a)(4)(F), including a report of the disciplinary action taken against the officer or employee who was primarily responsible for improperly withholding records or an explanation of why disciplinary action was not taken;

(5) a copy of every rule made by such agency regarding this section;

(6) a copy of the fee schedule and the total amount of fees collected by the agency for making records available under this section; and

(7) such other information as indicates efforts to administer fully this section.

The Attorney General shall submit an annual report on or before March 1 of each calendar year which shall include for the prior calendar year a listing of the number of cases arising under this section, the exemption involved in each case, the disposition of such case, and the cost, fees, and penalties assessed under subsection (a)(4)(E), (F), and (G). Such report shall also include a description of the efforts undertaken by the Department of Justice to encourage agency compliance with this section.

(e) For purposes of this section, the term 'agency' as defined in section 551(1) of this title includes any executive department, military department, Government corporation, Government controlled corporation, or other establishment in the executive branch of the Government (including the Executive Office of the President), or any independent regulatory agency.

# APPENDIX B

## PRIVACY ACT

### Public Law 93-579:
### The Privacy Act of 1974

Be it enacted by the Senate and House of Representatives of the United States of America in Congress assembled, That this Act may be cited as the "Privacy Act of 1974."

Sec. 2.

(a)    The Congress finds that—
    (1)    the privacy of an individual is directly affected by the collection, maintenance, use, and dissemination of personal information by Federal agencies;
    (2)    the increasing use of computers and sophisticated information technology, while essential to the efficient operations of the Government, has greatly magnified the harm to individual privacy that can occur from any collection, maintenance, use, or dissemination of personal information;
    (3)    the opportunities for an individual to secure employment, insurance, and credit, and his right to due process, and other legal protections are endangered by the misuse of certain information systems;
    (4)    the right to privacy is a personal and fundamental right protected by the Constitution of the United States; and
    (5)    in order to protect the privacy of individuals identified in information systems maintained by Federal agencies, it is necessary and proper for the Congress to regulate the collection, maintenance, use, and dissemination of information by such agencies.

(b)    The purpose of this Act is to provide certain safeguards for an individual against an invasion of personal privacy by requiring Federal agencies, except as otherwise provided by law, to—
    (1)    permit an individual to determine what records pertaining to him are collected, maintained, used, or disseminated by such agencies;
    (2)    permit an individual to prevent records pertaining to him obtained by such agencies for a particular purpose from being used or made available for another purpose without his consent;

(3) permit an individual to gain access to information pertaining to him in Federal agency records, to have a copy made of all or any portion thereof, and to correct or amend such records;

(4) collect, maintain, use, or disseminate any record of identifiable personal information in a manner that assures that such action is for a necessary and lawful purpose, that the information is current and accurate for its intended use, and that adequate safeguards are provided to prevent misuse of such information;

(5) permit exemptions from the requirements with respect to records provided in this Act only in those cases where there is an important public policy need for such exemption as has been determined by specific statutory authority; and

(6) be subject to civil suit for any damages which occur as a result of willful or intentional action which violates any individual's rights under this Act.

Sec. 3.

Title 5, United States Code, is amended by adding after section 552 the following new section:

"552a. Records maintained on individuals

"(a) DEFINITIONS. - For purposes of this section—

"(1) the term 'agency' means agency as defined in section 552(e) of this title;

"(2) the term 'individual' means a citizen of the United States or an alien lawfully admitted for permanent residence;

"(3) the term 'maintain' includes maintain, collect, use, or disseminate;

"(4) the term 'record' means any item, collection, or grouping of information about an individual that is maintained by an agency, including, but not limited to, his education, financial transactions, medical history, and criminal or employment history and that contains his name, or the identifying number, symbol, or other identifying particular assigned to the individual, such as a finger or voice print or a photograph;

"(5) the term 'system of records' means a group of any records under the control of any agency from which information is retrieved by the name of the individual or by some identifying number, symbol, or other identifying particular assigned to the individual;

"(6) the term 'statistical record' means a record in a system of records maintained for statistical research or reporting purposes only and not used in whole or in part in making any determination about an identifiable individual, except as provided by section 8 of title 13; and

"(7) the term 'routine use' means, with respect to the disclosure of a record, the use of such record for a purpose which is compatible with the purpose for which it was collected.

"(b) CONDITIONS OF DISCLOSURE. - No agency shall disclose any record which is contained in a system of records by any means of communication to any person, or to another agency, except pursuant to a written request by, or with the prior consent of, the individual to whom the record pertains, unless disclosure of the record would be—

"(1) to those officers and employees of the agency which maintains the record who have a need for the record in the performance of their duties;

"(2) required under section 552 of this title;

"(3) for a routine use as defined in subsection (a)(7) of this section and described under subsection (e)(4)(D) of this section;

"(4) to the Bureau of the Census for purposes of planning or carrying out a census of survey or related activity pursuant to the provisions of title 13;

"(5) to a recipient who has provided the agency with advance adequate written assurance that the record will be used solely as a statistical research or reporting record, and the record is to be transferred in a form that is not individually identifiable;

"(6) to the National Archives of the United States as a record which has sufficient historical or other value to warrant its continued preservation by the United States Government, or for evaluation by the Administrator of General Services or his designee to determine whether the record has such value;

"(7) to another agency or to an instrumentality of any governmental jurisdiction within or under the control of the United States for a civil or criminal law enforcement activity if the activity is authorized by law, and if the head of the agency or instrumentality has made a written request to the agency which maintains the record specifying the particular portion desired and the law enforcement activity for which the record is sought;

"(8) to a person pursuant to a showing of compelling circumstances affecting the health or safety of an individual if upon such disclosure notification is transmitted to the last known address of such individual;

"(9) to either House of Congress, or, to the extent of matter within its jurisdiction, any committee or subcommittee thereof, any joint committee of Congress or subcommittee of any such joint committee;

"(10) to the Comptroller General, or any of his authorized representatives, in the course of the performance of the duties of the General Accounting Office; or

"(11) pursuant to the order of a court of competent jurisdiction.

"(c) ACCOUNTING OF CERTAIN DISCLOSURES.—Each agency, with respect to each system of records under its control, shall—

"(1) except for disclosures made under subsections (b)(1) or (b)(2) of this section, keep an accurate accounting of—

"(A) the date, nature, and purpose of each disclosure of a record to any person or to another agency made under subsection (b) of this section; and

"(B) the name and address of the person or agency to whom the disclosure is made;

"(2) retain the accounting made under paragraph (1) of this subsection for at least five years or the life of the record, whichever is longer, after the disclosure for which the accounting is made;

"(3) except for disclosures made under subsection (b)(7) of this section, make the accounting made under paragraph (1) of this subsection available to the individual named in the record at his request; and

"(4) inform any person or other agency about any correction or notation of dispute made by the agency in accordance with subsection (d) of this section of any record that has been disclosed to the person or agency if an accounting of the disclosure was made.

"(d) ACCESS TO RECORDS.—Each agency that maintains a system of records shall—

"(1) upon request by any individual to gain access to his record or to any information pertaining to him which is contained in the system, permit him and upon his request, a person of his own choosing to accompany him, to review the record and have a copy made of all or any portion thereof in a form comprehensible to him, except that the agency may require the individual to furnish a written statement authorizing discussion of that individual's record in the accompanying person's presence;

"(2) permit the individual to request amendment of a record pertaining to him and—

"(A) not later than 10 days (excluding Saturdays, Sundays, and legal public holidays) after the date of receipt of such request, acknowledge in writing such receipt; and

"(B) promptly, either—

"(i) make any correction of any portion thereof which the individual believes is not accurate, relevant, timely, or complete; or

"(ii) inform the individual of its refusal to amend the record in accordance with his request, the reason for the refusal, the procedures established by the agency for the individual to request a review of that refusal by the head of the agency or an officer designated by the head of the agency, and the name and business address of that official;

"(3) permit the individual who disagrees with the refusal of the agency to amend his record to request a review of such refusal, and not later than 30 days (excluding Saturdays, Sundays, and legal public holidays) from the date on which the individual requests such review, complete such review and make a final determination unless, for good cause shown, the head of the agency extends such 30-day period; and if, after his review, the reviewing official also refuses to amend the record in accordance with the request, permit the individual to file with the agency a concise statement setting forth the reasons for his disagreement with the refusal of the agency, and notify the individual of the provisions for judicial review of the reviewing official's determination under subsection (g)(1)(A) of this section;

"(4) in any disclosure, containing information about which the individual has filed a statement of disagreement, occurring after the filing of the statement under paragraph (3) of this subsection, clearly note any portion of the record which is disputed and provide copies of the statement and, if the agency deems it appropriate, copies of a concise statement of the reasons of the agency for not making the amendments requested, to persons or other agencies to whom the disputed record has been disclosed; and

"(5) nothing in this section shall allow an individual access to any information compiled in reasonable anticipation of a civil action or proceeding.

"(e) AGENCY REQUIREMENTS.—Each agency that maintains a system of records shall—

"(1) maintain in its records only such information about an individual as is relevant and necessary to accomplish a purpose of the agency required to be accomplished by statute or by executive order of the President;

"(2) collect information to the greatest extent practicable directly from the subject individual when the information may result in adverse determinations about an individual's rights, benefits, and privileges under Federal programs;

"(3) inform each individual whom it asks to supply information, on the form which it uses to collect the information or on a separate form that can be retained by the individual—

"(A) the authority (whether granted by statute, or by executive order of the President) which authorizes the solicitation of the information and whether disclosure of such information is mandatory or voluntary;

"(B) the principal purpose or purposes for which the information is intended to be used;

"(C) the routine uses which may be made of the information, as published pursuant to paragraph (4)(D) of this subsection; and

"(D) the effects on him, if any, of not providing all or any part of the requested information;

"(4) subject to the provisions of paragraph (11) of this subsection, publish in the *Federal Register* at least annually a notice of the existence and character of the system of records, which notice shall include—

"(A) the name and location of the system;

"(B) the categories of individuals on whom records are maintained in the system;

"(C) the categories of records maintained in the system;

"(D) each routine use of the records contained in the system, including the categories of users and the purpose of such use;

"(E) the policies and practices of the agency regarding storage, retrievability, access controls, retention, and disposal of the records;

"(F) the title and business address of the agency official who is responsible for the system of records;

"(G) the agency procedures whereby an individual can be notified at his request if the system of records contains a record pertaining to him;

"(H) the agency procedures whereby an individual can be notified at his request how he can gain access to any record pertaining to him contained in the system of records, and how he can contest its content; and

"(I) the categories of sources of records in the system;

"(5) maintain all records which are used by the agency in making any determination about any individual with such accuracy, relevance, timeliness, and completeness as is reasonably necessary to assure fairness to the individual in the determination;

"(6) prior to disseminating any record about an individual to any person other than an agency, unless the dissemination is made pursuant to subsection (b)(2) of this section, make reasonable efforts to assure that such records are accurate, complete, timely, and relevant for agency purposes;

"(7) maintain no record describing how any individual exercises rights guaranteed by the First Amendment unless expressly authorized by statute or by the individual about whom the record is maintained or unless pertinent to and within the scope of an authorized law enforcement activity;

"(8) make reasonable efforts to serve notice on an individual when any record on such individual is made available to any person under compulsory legal process when such process becomes a matter of public record;

"(9) establish rules of conduct for persons involved in the design, development, operation, or maintenance of any system of records, or in maintaining any record, and instruct each such person with respect to such rules and the requirements of this section, including any other rules and procedures adopted pursuant to this section and the penalties for noncompliance;

"(10) establish appropriate administrative, technical, and physical safeguards to insure the security and confidentiality of records and to protect against any anticipated threats or hazards to their security or integrity which could result in substantial harm, embarrassment, inconvenience, or unfairness to any individual on whom information is maintained; and

"(11) at least 30 days prior to publication of information under paragraph (4)(D) of this subsection, publish in the *Federal Register* notice of any new use or intended use of the information in the system, and provide an opportunity for interested persons to submit written data, views, or arguments to the agency.

"(f) AGENCY RULES.—In order to carry out the provisions of this section, each agency that maintains a system of records shall promulgate rules, in accordance with the requirements (including general notice) of section 553 of this title, which shall—

"(1) establish procedures whereby an individual can be notified in response to his request if any system of records named by the individual contains a record pertaining to him;

"(2) define reasonable times, places, and requirements for identifying an individual who requests his record or information pertaining to him before the agency shall make the record or information available to the individual;

"(3) establish procedures for the disclosure to an individual upon his request of his record or information pertaining to him, including special procedure, if deemed necessary, for the disclosure to an individual of medical records, including psychological records, pertaining to him;

"(4) establish procedures for reviewing a request from an individual concerning the amendment of any record or information pertaining to the individual, for making a determination on the request, for an appeal within the agency of an initial adverse agency determination, and for whatever additional means may be necessary for each individual to be able to exercise fully his rights under this section; and

"(5) establish fees to be charged, if any, to any individual for making copies of his record, excluding the cost of any search for and review of the record.

The Office of the Federal Register shall annually compile and publish the rules promulgated under this subsection and agency notices published under subsection (e)(4) of this section in a form available to the public at low cost.

"(g) —

"(1) CIVIL REMEDIES.—Whenever any agency

"(A) makes a determination under subsection (d)(3) of this

section not to amend an individual's record in accordance with his request, or fails to make such review in conformity with that subsection;

"(B) refuses to comply with an individual request under subsection (d)(1) of this section;

"(C) fails to maintain any record concerning any individual with such accuracy, relevance, timeliness, and completeness as is necessary to assure fairness in any determination relating to the qualifications, character, rights, or opportunities of, or benefits to the individual that may be made on the basis of such record, and consequently a determination is made which is adverse to the individual; or

"(D) fails to comply with any other provision of this section, or any rule promulgated thereunder, in such a way as to have an adverse effect on an individual,

the individual may bring a civil action against the agency, and the district courts of the United States shall have jurisdiction in the matters under the provisions of this subsection.

"(2) —

"(A) In any suit brought under the provisions of subsection (g)(1)(A) of this section, the court may order the agency to amend the individual's record in accordance with his request or in such other way as the court may direct. In such a case the court shall determine the matter *de novo*.

"(B) The court may assess against the United States reasonable attorney fees and other litigation costs reasonably incurred in any case under this paragraph in which the complainant has substantially prevailed.

"(3) —

"(A) In any suit brought under the provisions of subsection (g)(1)(B) of this section, the court may enjoin the agency from withholding the records and order the production to the complainant of any agency records improperly withheld from him. In such a case the court shall determine the matter *de novo*, and may examine the contents of any agency records *in camera* to determine whether the records or any portion thereof may be withheld under any of the exemptions set forth in subsection (k) of this section, and the burden is on the agency to sustain its action.

"(B) The court may assess against the United States reasonable attorney fees and other litigation costs reasonably incurred in any case under this paragraph in which the complainant has substantially prevailed.

"(4) In any suit brought under the provisions of subsection (g)(1)(C) or (D) of this section in which the court determines that the agency acted in a manner which was intentional or willful, the United States shall be liable to the individual in an amount equal to the sum of—

"(A) actual damages sustained by the individual as a result of the refusal or failure, but in no case shall a person entitled to recovery receive less than the sum of $1,000; and

"(B) the costs of the action together with reasonable attorney fees as determined by the court.

"(5) An action to enforce any liability created under this section may be brought in the district court of the United States in the district in which the complainant resides, or has his principal place of business, or in which the agency records are situated, or in the District of Columbia, without regard to the amount in controversy, within two years from the date on which the cause of action arises, except that where any agency has materially and willfully misrepresented any information required under this section to be disclosed to an individual and the information so misrepresented is material to establishment of liability of the agency to the individual under this section, the action may be brought at any time within two years after discovery by the individual of the misrepresentation. Nothing in this section shall be construed to authorize any civil action by reason of any injury sustained as the result of a disclosure of a record prior to the effective date of this section.

"(h) RIGHTS OF LEGAL GUARDIANS.—For the purposes of this section, the parent of any minor, or the legal guardian of any individual who has been declared to be incompetent due to physical or mental incapacity or age by a court of competent jurisdiction, may act on behalf of the individual.

"(i) —

"(1) CRIMINAL PENALTIES.—Any officer or employee of an agency, who by virtue of his employment or official position, has possession of, or access to, agency records which contain individually identifiable information the disclosure of which is prohibited by this section or by rules or regulations established thereunder, and who knowing that disclosure of the specific material is so prohibited, willfully discloses the material in any manner to any person or agency not entitled to receive it, shall be guilty of a misdemeanor and fined not more than $5,000.

"(2) Any officer or employee of any agency who willfully maintains a system of records without meeting the notice requirements of subsection (e)(4) of this section shall be guilty of a misdemeanor and fined not more than $5,000.

"(3) Any person who knowingly and willfully requests or obtains any record concerning an individual from an agency under false pretenses be guilty of a misdemeanor and fined not more than $5,000.

"(j) GENERAL EXEMPTIONS.—The head of any agency may promulgate rules, in accordance with the requirements (including general notice) of sections 553(b)(1), (2), and (3), (c), and (e) of this title, to exempt any system of records within the agency from any part of this section except subsections (b), (c)(1) and (2), (e)(4)(A) through (F), (e)(6), (7), (9), (10), and (11), and (i) if the system of records is—

"(1) maintained by the Central Intelligence Agency; or

"(2) maintained by an agency or component thereof which performs as its principal function any activity pertaining to the enforcement of criminal laws, including police efforts to prevent, control, or reduce crime or to apprehend criminals, and the activities of prosecutors, courts, correctional, probation, pardon, or parole authorities, and which consists of (A) information compiled for the purpose of identifying individual criminal offenders and alleged offenders and consisting only of identifying data and notations of arrests, the nature and disposition of criminal charges, sentencing, confinement, release, and parole and probation status; (B) information compiled for the purpose of a criminal investigation, including reports of informants and investigators, and associated with an identifiable individual; or (C) reports identifiable to an individual compiled at any stage of the process of enforcement of criminal laws from arrest or indictment through release from supervision.

At the time rules are adopted under this subsection, the agency shall include in the statement required under section 553(c) of this title, the reasons why the system of records is to be exempted from a provision of this section.

"(k) SPECIFIC EXEMPTIONS.—The head of any agency may promulgate rules, in accordance with the requirements (including general notice) of sections 553(b)(1), (2), and (3), (c), and (e) of this title, to exempt any system of records within the agency from subsections (c)(3), (d), (e)(1), (e)(4)(G), (H), and (I) and (f) of this section if the system of records is—

"(1) subject to the provisions of section 552(b)(1) of this title;

"(2) investigatory material compiled for law enforcement purposes, other than material within the scope of subsection (j)(2) of this section: *Provided, however*, That if any individual is denied any right, privilege, or benefit that he would otherwise be entitled by Federal Law, or for which he would otherwise be eligible, as a result of the maintenance of such material, such material shall be provided to such individual, except to the extent that the disclosure of such material would reveal the identity of a source who furnished information to the

Government under an express promise that the identity of the source would be held in confidence, or, prior to the effective date of this section, under an implied promise that the identity of the source would be held in confidence;

"(3) maintained in connection with providing protective services to the President of the United States or other individuals pursuant to Section 3056 of title 18;

"(4) required by statute to be maintained and used solely as statistical records;

"(5) investigatory material compiled solely for the purpose of determining suitability, eligibility, or qualifications for Federal civilian employment, military service, Federal contracts, or access to classified information, but only to the extent that the disclosure of such material would reveal the identity of a source who furnished information to the Government under an express promise that the identity of the source would be held in confidence, or, prior to the effective date of this section, under an implied promise that the identity of the source would be held in confidence;

"(6) testing or examination material used solely to determine individual qualifications for appointment or promotion in the Federal service the disclosure of which would compromise the objectivity or fairness of the testing or examination process; or

"(7) evaluation material used to determine potential for promotion in the armed services, but only to the extent that the disclosure of such material would reveal the identity of a source who furnished information to the Government under an express promise that the identity of the source would be held in confidence, or, prior to the effective date of this section, under an implied promise that the identity of the source would be held in confidence.

At the time rules are adopted under this subsection, the agency shall include in the statement required under section 553(c) of this title, the reasons why the system of records is to be exempted from a provision of this section.

"(l) ARCHIVAL RECORDS.—

"(1) Each agency record which is accepted by the Administrator of General Services for storage, processing, and servicing in accordance with section 3103 of title 44 shall, for the purposes of this section, be considered to be maintained by the agency which deposited the record and shall be subject to the provisions of this section. The Administrator of General Services shall not disclose the record except to the agency which maintains the record, or under rules established by that agency which are not inconsistent with the provisions of this section.

"(2) Each agency record pertaining to an identifiable individual which was transferred to the National Archives of the United States as a record which has sufficient historical or other value to warrant its continued preservation by the United States Government, prior to the effective date of this section, shall, for the purposes of this section, be considered to be maintained by the National Archives and shall not be subject to the provisions of this section, except that a statement generally describing such records (modeled after the requirements relating to records subject to subsections (e)(4)(A) through (G) of this section) shall be published in the *Federal Register*.

"(3) Each agency record pertaining to an identifiable individual which is transferred to the National Archives of the United States as a record which has sufficient historical or other value to warrant its continued preservation by the United States Government, on or after the effective date of this section, shall, for the purposes of this section, be considered to be maintained by the National Archives and shall be exempt from the requirements of this section except subsections (e)(4)(A) through (G) and (e)(9) of this section.

"(m) GOVERNMENT CONTRACTORS.—When an agency provides by a contract for the operation by or on behalf of the agency of a system of records to accomplish an agency function, the agency shall, consistent with its authority, cause the requirements of this section to be applied to such system. For purposes of subsection (i) of this section any such contractor and any employee of such contractor, if such contract is agreed to on or after the effective date of this section, shall be considered to be an employee of an agency.

"(n) MAILING LISTS.—An individual's name and address may not be sold or rented by an agency unless such action is specifically authorized by law. This provision shall not be construed to require the withholding of names and addresses otherwise permitted to be made public.

"(o) REPORT ON NEW SYSTEMS.—Each agency shall provide adequate advance notice to Congress and the Office of Management and Budget of any proposal to establish or alter any system of records in order to permit an evaluation of the probable or potential effect of such proposal on the privacy and other personal or property rights of individuals or the disclosure of information relating to such individuals, and its effect on the the preservation of the constitutional principles of federalism and separation of powers.

"(p) ANNUAL REPORT.—The President shall submit to the Speaker of the House and the President of the Senate, by June 30 of each calendar year, a consolidated report, separately listing for each Federal agency the number of records contained in any system of records which were exempted from the application of this section under the provisions of subsections (j) and (k) of this section during the preceding calendar year, and the reasons for the exemptions, and such other information as indicates efforts to administer fully this section.

"(q) EFFECT OF OTHER LAWS.—No agency shall rely on any exemption contained in section 552 of this title to withhold from an individual any record which is otherwise accessible to such individual under the provisions of this section."

Sec. 4.

The Chapter analysis of chapter 5 of title 5, United States Code, is amended by inserting:

"552a. Records about individuals."

immediately below:

"552. Public information; agency rules, opinions, orders, and proceedings.".

[Section 5 of the Privacy Act established a Privacy Protection Study Commission for a period of two years. Its term has now expired. Among other things, the Commission was charged with the responsibility of assessing the effectiveness of privacy protections throughout the society. In July 1977, it issued a report entitled "Personal Privacy in an Information Society" which proposed a series of recommendations directed toward safeguarding personal privacy in both the public and private sector. This report can be obtained from the Superintendent of Documents, Government Printing Office, Washington, D.C. 20420 for a charge of $5.]

Sec. 6.

The Office of Management and Budget shall—

(1) develop guidelines and regulations for the use of agencies in implementing the provisions of section 552a of title 5, United States Code, as added by section 3 of this Act; and

(2) provide continuing assistance to and oversight of the implementation of the provisions of such section by agencies.

Sec. 7.

(a) —

    (1)  It shall be unlawful for any Federal, State or local government agency to deny to any individual any right, benefit, or privilege provided by law because of such individual's refusal to disclose his social security account number.

    (2)  The provisions of paragraph (1) of this subsection shall not apply with respect to—

        (A)  any disclosure which is required by Federal statute, or

        (B)  the disclosure of a social security number to any Federal, State, or local agency maintaining a system of records in existence and operating before January 1, 1975, if such disclosure was required under statute or regulation adopted prior to such date to verify the identity of an individual.

(b)  Any Federal, State, or local government agency which requests an individual to disclose his social security number to any Federal, State, or local agency maintaining a system of records in existence and operating before January 1, 1975, if such disclosure was required under statute or regulation adopted prior to such date to verify the identity of an individual.

(b)  Any Federal, State, or local government agency which requests an individual to disclose his social security account number shall inform that individual whether that disclosure is mandatory or voluntary, by what statutory or other authority such number is solicited, and what uses will be made of it.

Sec. 8.

The provisions of this Act shall be effective on and after the date of enactment, except that the amendments made by section 3 and 4 shall become effective 270 days following the day on which this Act is enacted.

Sec. 9.

There is authorized to be appropriated to carry out the provisions of section 5 of this Act for fiscal years 1975, 1976, and 1977 the sum of $1,500,000, except that not more than $750,000 may be expended during any such fiscal year.

Approved December 31, 1974

# APPENDIX C

## Recent FOIA Requests Submitted to
## Federal Trade Commission

This appendix includes copies of four requests submitted to the Federal Trade Commission and the FTC's response thereto. Two of these requests include appeals of agency denial of the information requested.

Appendix D to follow gives an example of a denial of information and an appeal of this denial to U.S. district courts.

The examples given here are included only for purposes of illustration and do not indicate any indorsement of the parties or issues involved.

Summaries of the FOIA requests listed below are as follows:

(1) FTC files re studies or investigations concerning requirement that warning labels appear on consumer products. *Req. by:* Gary Komarow, Esq. of Loomis, Owen et al, Washington, D.C. Granted in part. 4/14/81. Exemptions: (b)(5), inter-intra agency memoranda; (b)(7)(A), enforcement proceedings. (See page 90.)

(2) Information re K Mart Enterprises Inc. and its use of comparative advertising. *Req. by:* Douglas J. Wood, Esq., of Hall, Dickler et al, New York, N.Y. Granted in part. 1/14/81. Exemptions: (b)(3), specifically exempted by statute; (b)(4), trade secrets; et al. (See page 93).

(3) Information re problems associated with 400 cubic-inch engine used in 1979 Chevrolet Suburban vehicle. *Req. by:* Steve Smith, Esq. of Dillon & Giesnschlag, Bryan, Tex. Granted in part. 5/29/81. Exemption: (b)(7)(A), enforcement proceedings. (See page 99).

(4) Studies of Japanese automobile industry, undertaken during course of FTC's investigation of U.S. automobile industry. *Req. by:* Dennis A. Addelson, Esq., of Rivkin, Sherman & Levy, Washington, D.C. Granted in part. 5/7/81. Exemption: (b)(5), inter-intra agency memoranda. (See page 101).

*Law Offices*

## Loomis, Owen, Fellman & Howe

*(formerly Counihan, Casey & Loomis)*

*2020 K Street, N. W.*

*Washington, D. C. 20006*

*202 296-5680*

John E. Loomis
Stephen F. Owen, Jr.
Steven John Fellman
William H. Howe
James E. Anderson
Henry A. Hart
Timothy J. Parsons
Richard A. Stoyer

Donald M. Counihan
*1913-1969*
E. Riley Casey
*1923-1971*

J. R. Pat Gorman
Elmer F. Bennett
*Counsel*

March 16, 1981

Freedom of Information Act Request
Office of the Secretary
Federal Trade Commission
6th Street & Pennsylvania Ave., N.W.
Washington, D.C.    20580

Gentlemen:

> Re:   Freedom of Information
>       Act Request

   Pursuant to the Freedom of Information Act, 5 U.S.C. § 552, and the regulations promulgated thereunder by FTC at C.F.R. Part 4, we hereby request that you provide us with the following documents:

> Copies of all records in FTC's files pertaining to any studies, investigations, or inquiries, formal or informal, conducted by or on behalf of FTC, or known to exist by FTC personnel, concerning the effects of requiring warning labels, warning statements, or any other type of warnings or cautionary notices in conjunction with the sale or manufacture of any form of consumer product, regardless of whether or not the sale or manufacture of such product is subject to regulation by FTC.

   Please telephone the undersigned as soon as these documents are available, and notify the undersigned if the expense of complying with this request exceeds $100.

   Thank you for your cooperation.

                    Very truly yours,

                    LOOMIS, OWEN, FELLMAN & HOWE

                    Gary Komarow

**FEDERAL TRADE COMMISSION**
WASHINGTON, D. C. 20580

OFFICE OF THE SECRETARY

APR 1 4 1981

Gary Komarow, Esquire
Loomis, Owen, Fellman & Howe
2020 K Street, N.W.
Washington, D.C.  20006

      Re:  Freedom of Information Act Request
            Warning Labels
            FOIA No. 81-0249

Dear Mr. Komarow:

      This is in response to your letter of March 16, 1981, which requests information concerning the effects of requiring warning labels.

      Your request is granted in part.  You are granted access to documents consisting of the following:

        (a)  Publicity concerning the FTC's antacid TRR.

        (b)  Proprietary Association "Hearing highlights" from antacid TRR.

        (c)  Paper by Houston and Rothschild.

        (d)  Studies on warning effectiveness.

        (e)  Report on the cigarette health.

      Additional responsive documents can be located from our Public Reference Branch, Room 130, telephone number, 523-3598.  These addtional documents are described as follows:

        (a)  Analgesics cases on docket matters: D 8918 - (Bristol Meyer), D 8917 - Sterling Drug and D 8919.

        (b)  Antacid Trade Rule Regulation - Public Record No. 215-56.

        (c)  Food & Drug Administration concerning tampons - 45 Fed. Reg. 69840 (October 21, 1980).

You are denied access to some of the materials responsive to your request because they are exempt from mandatory disclosure pursuant to 5 U.S.C. Section 552 subsections (b)(5) and (b)(7)(A). Subsection (b)(5) is being invoked for intra-agency staff memoranda which would not be available to a party other than an agency in litigation with the Commission and the Commissioner's materials. Subsection (b)(7)(A) is being invoked to protect investigatory records compiled for law enforcement purposes, but only to the extent that the production of such records would interfere with enforcement proceedings.

Pursuant to 5 U.S.C. Section 552(a)(4)(A) you are being charged $65.24 for duplication fees. Please remit this amount at your earliest convenience, payable to the Treasury of the United States to Division of Budget and Finance, Room 766, Federal Trade Commission, Washington, D.C. 20580. Enclosed are the documents being provided to you.

You may petition the Commission for access to the information being withheld within (30) days. You may petition either because you believe that the material is not exempt under the law, or because you believe that the Commission should exercise its discretion and release the information notwithstanding its exempt status. If requesting discretionary release, you should state your interest in the subject matter and the purpose for which it would be used if access is granted. Please include a copy of your original letter and this response with your appeal. The request should be addressed: Freedom of Information Act Appeal, Office of the General Counsel, Federal Trade Commission, Sixth Street and Pennsylvania Avenue, N.W., Washington, D.C. 20580.

Richard C. Foster is the official responsible for the partial denial of your request.

Sincerely,

Signed and Mailed

Carol M. Thomas
Secretary

Enclosures

# Hall, Dickler, Lawler, Kent & Howley

460 PARK AVENUE

NEW YORK, N. Y. 10022

AREA CODE 212 838-4600
CABLE "HALCASRO"

*FREEDOM OF INFORMATION SECTION*
*RECEIVED*
*DEC 18 1980*
*80-1725*
*FEDERAL TRADE COMMISSION*

December 15, 1980

Freedom of Information Act
    Officer
Federal Trade Commission
Washington, D.C.  20580

Dear Sir:

Pursuant to the Freedom of Information Act, please provide us with the following documents:

1. The consent order and complete file in the matter of K Mart Enterprises Inc., file number 7423155, docket number C-2553. We are specifically interested in any documents which pertain to the requirement that scientific testing maintain a minimum confidence level before results may be used to justify product claims whether made in comparative or non-comparative advertising.

2. Any agency documents or internal memoranda, reports, opinions, consent orders, consent agreements, complaints, or orders which pertain to the necessity that product claims be substantiated by research or testing that must maintain a minimum confidence level. Our interest is primarily directed to any agency materials which shed further light on the provisions in the K Mart Enterprises Inc. matter dealing with minimum confidence levels in surveys and tests.

Should there be any charge for the above, please invoice us accordingly. If you anticipate that such charges should exceed $250.00, please inform us prior to fulfilling our request.

Freedom of Information Act Officer
December 15, 1980
Page 2


Thank you for your cooperation.

Very truly yours,

HALL, DICKLER, LAWLER, KENT &
    HOWLEY

By _____
Douglas J. Wood

DJW:rt

**FEDERAL TRADE COMMISSION**
WASHINGTON. D. C. 20580

OFFICE OF THE SECRETARY

14 JAN 1981

Douglas J. Wood, Esquire
Hall, Dickler, Lawler, Kent &
   Howley
460 Park Avenue
New York, New York   10022

Re:   Freedom of Information Act Request
      K Mart Enterprises, Inc.
      FOIA Control Number 80-1725

Dear Mr. Wood:

This is in response to your letter of December 15, 1980
requesting information concerning K Mart Enterprises, Inc.,
and in particular, the requirement that scientific testing
maintain a minimum confidence level before results may be used
to justify product claims whether made in comparative or non-
comparative advertising.

It is my understanding that during your January 6, 1981
telephone conversation with John C. Summers, of the Freedom of
Information Branch, you limited your request to documents in
the K Mart Enterprises, Inc. investigation, C-2553, which discuss minimum confidence levels in scientific testing.

You are granted partial access to the material requested.
Portions of an internal Commission memoranda contain information
which was obtained by the Commission under compulsory process or
voluntarily in lieu thereof, in connection with an investigation,
a purpose of which was to determine whether any person may have
violated any provision of the laws administered by the Commission.
This information is exempt from disclosure under 5 U.S.C. section
552 (b)(3), by virtue of section 21(f) of the FTC Act, as amended,
15 U.S.C. section 57b-2.

The memorandum also contains trade secrets and confidential
commercial or financial information which the Commission is prohibited from publicly disclosing by section 6(f) of the FTC Act,
as amended.  In addition, this information is exempt from disclosure under FOIA Exemptions 3 and 4, 5 U.S.C. section 552
subsection (b)(3) and (b)(4).  See National Parks & Conservation
Ass'n v. Morton, 498 F.2d 765 (D.C. Cir. 1974).

Douglas J. Wood, Esquire                                    -2-


    Additional portions of this internal Commission memorandum
are being released to you as an act of discretion even though
they are exempt from disclosure under FOIA Exemption 5, 5 U.S.C.
section 552 (b)(5).  Enclosed, at no charge, are copies of all
accessible documents.

    You may petition the Commission for access to the material
which is being withheld within thirty (30) days.  You may petition either because you believe that the material is not exempt
under the law, or because you believe that the Commission should
exercise its discretion and release the information notwithstanding its exempt status.  If requesting discretionary release, you
should state your interest in the subject matter and the purpose
for which it would be used if access is granted.  Please include
a copy of your original letter and this response with your appeal.
Your request should be addressed:  Freedom of Information Act
Appeal, Office of the General Counsel, Federal Trade Commission,
Sixth Street and Pennsylvania Avenue, N.W., Washington, D.C.
20580.

    The undersigned is the sole official responsible for those
portions of your request which are denied.

                                    Sincerely,


                              SIGNED & MAILED

                              Carol M. Thomas
                              Secretary


Enclosures

LAW OFFICES

# HALL, DICKLER, LAWLER, KENT & HOWLEY

460 PARK AVENUE

NEW YORK, N. Y. 10022

AREA CODE 212 838-4600

CABLE "HALCASRO"

LEONARD W. HALL (1900-1979)
GERALD DICKLER
T. NEWMAN LAWLER
FELIX H. KENT
THOMAS R. AMLICKE
DAVID H. CARLIN
MILFORD FENSTER
SAMUEL J. FRIEDMAN
DAVID L. GOLDRICH
JOHN J. HAMILTON
WILLIAM L. MAHER
WILLIAM J. MARLOW
LANDIS OLESKER
PIERCE PALEY
RICHARD B. RODMAN
PAUL SARNO
MORTON A. SMITH
EDMUND S. WARTELS

JOSEPH CHASE
NORMAN L. FABER
NATALIE Z. HERTZ
ROBIN L. HIRSCH
GERALD W. JARRETT
DONALD M. KLEIN
JAMES F. LEHRBURGER
MICHAEL A. MEYERS
PAUL G. WHITBY
DOUGLAS J. WOOD

MORTIMOR S. GORDON
EDWIN McMAHON SINGER
COUNSEL
—
800 OLD COUNTRY ROAD
GARDEN CITY, N. Y. 11530
516 747-7000

WHITE PLAINS PLAZA
ONE NORTH BROADWAY
WHITE PLAINS, NEW YORK 10601
914 428-3232

January 22, 1981

Freedom of Information Act Appeal
Office of the General Counsel
Federal Trade Commission
Sixth Street and Pennsylvania
    Avenue, N.W.
Washington, D.C.  20580

> Re:  Freedom of Information Act Request
>      K Mart Enterprises, Inc.
>      FOIA Control Number 80-1725

Dear Sir:

This is to appeal your agency's refusal to release certain information pursuant to the above referenced Freedom of Information Act request.

A copy of my original letter, together with your agency's reply are enclosed herewith.

The purpose of this request was to secure information concerning the Commission's position on the required confidence levels, i.e., statistical significance projections of test data and surveys used to justify advertising claims.

This appeal is to request that you review the withheld material and release, on a discretionary basis, any further information dealing with the Commission's position on test or survey results.

Freedom of Information Act Appeal
January 22, 1981
Page 2


       Thank you in advance for your cooperation.

                     Very truly yours,

                 Douglas J. Wood

DJW:rt

Enclosures

LAW OFFICES

# DILLON & GIESENSCHLAG, P. C.

Metro Centre

3833 Texas Avenue

BRYAN, TEXAS 77801

May 11, 1981

Post Office Box 4067
713/846-1773

DON DILLON
TOM GIESENSCHLAG
SAM SHARP
BILL YOUNGKIN
STEVE SMITH
LARRY CATLIN
LARRY HOLT

Freedom of Information Act Request
Office of the Secretary
Federal Trade Commission
6th Street and Pennsylvania Ave. NW
Washington, D.C. 20580

    RE: 400 cubic-inch engines manufactured by General
        Motors, Chevrolet Motor Division and used in
        Suburban or similar vehicles in model year 1979

Gentlemen:

    I am attempting to document possible problems with
the 400 cubic-inch engine used in a 1979 Chevrolet Suburban
vehicle. The engine was probably manufactured by the Chevrolet Motor Division of GM.

    Please forward any information you might have regarding
mechanical problems that have been complained of in connection
with this particular engine.

    We stand ready to pay all reasonable costs in connection
with this request.

                Sincerely yours,

                DILLON & GIESENSCHLAG, P.C.

                Steve Smith

SLS/bb

**FEDERAL TRADE COMMISSION**
WASHINGTON, D. C. 20580

OFFICE OF THE SECRETARY

Steve Smith, Esquire                                    MAY 29 1981
Dillon & Giesenschlag, P.C.
Metro Centre
3833 Texas Avenue
Bryan, Texas  77801

      Re:  Freedom of Information Act Request
          1979 Chevrolet Suburban
          FOIA No. 81-0450

Dear Mr. Smith:

    This is in response to your letter of May 11, 1981, in which
you requested access to information concerning problems with the
400 cubic-inch engine used in a 1979 Chevrolet Suburban vehicle.

    Your request is granted in part.  You are granted access to
portions of various letters of consumer complaint.  To obtain the
accessible materials, you may wish to contact Brenda Doudrava,
Attorney, Cleveland Regional Office, Suite 500 - Mall Building,
118 St. Clair Avenue, Cleveland, Ohio 44114, telephone numbers
(commercial) 216 522-4207 or (FTS) 293-4207.

    You are denied access to portions of various letters of consumer
complaint.  These documents are being withheld because they are
exempt from mandatory disclosure pursuant to 5 U.S.C. Section 552
subsection (b)(7)(A).  Subsection (b)(7)(A) is being invoked to
protect investigatory records compiled for law enforcement purposes,
but only to the extent that the production of such records would
interfere with enforcement proceedings.

    You may petition the Commission for access to the information
being withheld within (30) days.  You may petition either because
you believe that the material is not exempt under the law, or
because you believe that the Commission should exercise its
discretion and release the information notwithstanding its exempt
status.  If requesting discretionary release, you should state your

# RIVKIN SHERMAN AND LEVY

COUNSELLORS AT LAW

DONALD H. RIVKIN
SAUL L. SHERMAN
JOSEPH LEVY
MILTON D. ANDREWS
JOSEPH S. KAPLAN
DONALD M. SCHWENTKER
ISAAC E. DRUKER
THOMAS A. GREENE*
ASHER S. LEVITSKY
ANDREW L. BERGER*
JOHN D. MILLER*

DENNIS A. ADELSON
CHARLES H. BAYAR
ALDEN J. BIANCHI
MARY CHRISTINE CARTY
RICHARD W. COHEN*
LORAINE F. GARDNER*
W. MICHAEL GARNER*
ALLEN S. KENYON*
LANCE E. TUNICK

*NOT ADMITTED IN DISTRICT OF COLUMBIA

900 17TH STREET, N. W.

WASHINGTON, D. C. 20006
(202) 347-6007
CABLE "DEJURIBUS WASHINGTON"
TELEX 892615
RAPIFAX (202) 296-8930

750 THIRD AVENUE
NEW YORK, N.Y. 10017
(212) 986-5220
CABLE "DEJURIBUS NEW YORK"
TELEX 147196

May 4, 1981

Freedom Of Information Act Request
Office of the Secretary
Federal Trade Commission
6th & Pennsylvania Avenue, N.W.
Washington, D.C. 20580

                                        Freedom of Information Act Request

Dear Sir or Madam:

Pursuant to the Freedom of Information Act, as amended, 5 U.S.C. §552, and 16 C.F.R. §4.11, I request a copy of all consultant studies of the Japanese automobile industry conducted in connection with the FTC's automobile industry investigation. This is the same material that was the subject of Request No. 81-0338 of April 7, 1981 by Steptoe and Johnson.

I am willing to pay fees up to $25.00. If you anticipate higher fees, please call me for authorization. I await your reply within ten working days.

Sincerely,

RIVKIN SHERMAN and LEVY

Dennis A. Adelson

DAA:dlh

## FEDERAL TRADE COMMISSION
### WASHINGTON, D. C. 20580

**OFFICE OF THE SECRETARY**


Dennis A. Adelson, Esquire                    MAY 7   1981
Rivkin, Sherman and Levy
900 17th Street, N.W.
Washington, D.C.  20006

                Re:   Freedom of Information Act Request
                      Automobile Industry Studies
                      FOIA Control Number 81-0414

Dear Mr. Adelson:

    This is in response to your letter of May 4, 1981 request-
ing copies of various studies of the Japanese automobile
industry, undertaken during the course of the Commission's
investigation of the United States automobile industry,
initiated in 1976.

    You are denied access to the material requested.  These
materials are exempt from mandatory disclosure pursuant to
5 U.S.C. section 552 (b)(5).  Subsection (b)(5) is being
invoked to withhold the studies, since they constitute
attorney work product.

    You may petition the Commission for access to the material
which is being withheld within thirty (30) days.  You may petition either because you believe that the material is not exempt
under the law, or because you believe that the Commission should
exercise its discretion and release the information notwithstanding its exempt status.  If requesting discretionary release,
you should state your interest in the subject matter and the
purpose for which it would be used if access is granted.  Please
include a copy of your original letter and this response with
your appeal.  The request should be addressed:  Freedom of
Information Act Appeal, Office of the General Counsel, Federal
Trade Commission, Sixth Street and Pennsylvania Avenue, N.W.,
Washington, D.C.  20580.

    The undersigned is the sole official responsible for the
denial of your request.

                                    Sincerely,

                              | **Signed and Mailed** |


                                    Carol M. Thomas
                                    Secretary

# RIVKIN SHERMAN AND LEVY

COUNSELLORS AT LAW

DONALD H. RIVKIN
SAUL L. SHERMAN
JOSEPH LEVY
MILTON D. ANDREWS
DONALD M. SCHWENTKER
ISAAC E. DRUKER
THOMAS A. GREENE*
ASHER S. LEVITSKY
ANDREW L. BERGER*
JOHN D. MILLER*

DENNIS A. ADELSON
CHARLES H. BAYAR
JOSEPH L. BUCKLEY*
MARY CHRISTINE CARTY
RICHARD W. COHEN*
LORAINE F. GARDNER*
W. MICHAEL GARNER*
ALLEN S. KENYON*
LANCE E. TUNICK

*NOT ADMITTED IN DISTRICT OF COLUMBIA

900 17TH STREET, N. W.

WASHINGTON, D. C. 20006

(202) 347-6007

CABLE "DEJURIBUS WASHINGTON"

TELEX 892615

RAPIFAX (202) 296-8930

—

750 THIRD AVENUE

NEW YORK, N. Y. 10017

(212) 986-5220

CABLE "DEJURIBUS NEW YORK"

TELEX 147196

May 18, 1981

Freedom of Information Act Appeal
Office of the General Counsel
Federal Trade Commission
6th & Pennsylvania Avenue, N.W.
Washington, D.C. 20580

                                    Automobile Industry Studies
                                    FOIA Control Number 81-0414

Dear Sir or Madam:

Pursuant to 16 C.F.R. §4.11(a)(2), we hereby appeal the denial of
the above-referenced Freedom of Information Act request. This
request was made by this firm on May 4, 1981. A copy of the request
is attached hereto as Exhibit A. A copy of the denial of this
request dated May 7, 1981 is attached hereto as Exhibit B.

The request sought the disclosure of consultant studies of the
Japanese automobile industry. The request was denied on the basis
of Exemption 5 of the FOIA, 5 U.S.C. §552(b)(5). The agency claimed
the studies were subject to protection under the attorney work
product privilege. We believe this exemption was incorrectly used
as the basis for denying the release of part or all of these
studies. Use of this exemption was also not properly substantiated
or even explained in the FTC's notice of denial. However, even if a
proper legal basis exists for withholding the studies, they should
be disclosed as a matter of agency discretion.

1.   The Use Of Exemption 5 To Deny Disclosure Has Not Been
     Substantiated By The FTC

Exemption 5 permits records to be withheld if they would not be
routinely available to a party in litigation with the agency.
5 U.S.C. §552(b)(5). This language has been held to create an

Federal Trade Commission
May 18, 1981
Page 2


exemption roughly equivalent to the scope of those privileges
recognized in discovery under Rule 26 of the Federal Rules of Civil
Procedure.  EPA v. Mink, 410 U.S. 73,86 (1973).  The attorney work
product privilege is one of those privileges which has been
incorporated into Exemption 5.  In both the civil discovery and FOIA
contexts, the privilege has been held to encompass documents
prepared by or at the request of an attorney, in connection with or
in contemplation of litigation.  See, e.g. Sterling Drug, Inc. v.
Harris, 488 F.Supp 1019,1026 (S.D.N.Y. 1980).

The agency, in its denial of our FOIA request, completely failed to
offer any explanation as to why the studies in question might fall
within the work product privilege.  It was not asserted that the
studies were prepared by attorneys.  Indeed, information available
to us indicates they were prepared by economic analysts, not
lawyers.  Neither did the agency state that the studies were
prepared at the request of agency attorneys.  It is quite possible
that the consultants who performed the studies were hired by
non-attorney staff members.  As such, the privilege would not
attach.  See Sterling, supra, at 1026.  If the studies were in fact
commissioned by attorneys, it is incumbent on the agency to name
them or their office and describe the circumstances of that
commission, so that appellant and the reviewing court can determine
if the privilege has been properly invoked.

The agency has also failed to identify the particular litigation in
connection with which these studies were prepared.  The existence or
imminency of such litigation is a necessary element of the
privilege.  It has been stated that

> "[A]t the very least some articulable claim, likely to lead to
> litigation, must have arisen....[T]he documents must at least
> have been prepared with a specific claim supported by concrete
> facts...."

Coastal States Gas Corp. v. D.O.E., 617 F.2d 854,865 (D.C.Cir.
1980).  The mere possibility of litigation is not sufficient to
claim the privilege.  Ibid. See also Jordan v. D.O.J. 591 F.2d 753
(D.C.Cir. 1978).  We know of no litigation, pending at or
contemplated by the FTC, dealing with the Japanese automobile
industry, or any other automobile industry.  The FTC's broad
automobile industry investigation has been formally closed without
ever approaching the point at which litigation was a serious
possibility.  It is also unlikely that studies like these, whose
apparent scope is very broad, would ever have been prepared for use
by the FTC in a non-safety related defects proceeding against a
particular company.  Rather, we suspect that the studies were
intended to provide background economic data and analysis for an
entire industry, which the agency could use to determine whether

Federal Trade Commission
May 18, 1981
Page 3


action in the form of a formal investigation, rulemaking or
litigation was warranted.  The studies presumably could just as
easily have remained in the files as background information only,
upon which no action would be taken.  The agency's use of these
studies is in apparent contrast to its earlier use of an analysis of
economic theories and litigation strategies to be used in a
proceeding against the oil industry.  In Exxon Corp. v. F.T.C., 466
F.Supp. 1088 (D.D.C. 1978), the invocation of the work product
privilege as to this study was upheld because it was prepared at the
direction of agency attorneys after a complaint had been issued.
Unless the agency comes forward to explain the origin, nature and
purpose of the studies we have requested, it cannot properly invoke
the work product privilege.


2.    The FTC Has Not Met Its Burden Of Specifying Which Material Is
      Exempt And Which Is Not

Section 552(b) of Title 5, U.S.C. requires the FTC to provide

      "Any reasonably segregable portion of a record...after deletion
      of the portions which are exempt under this subsection."

The FTC has made no attempt to identify and disclose any information
in the reports which does not fall within the broad sweep of
Exemption 5.  It is incumbent upon the FTC to do so.  We seriously
doubt that the FTC could not find even a single piece of disclosable
material in either study.  As stated in Vaughn v. Rosen, 484 F.2d
820 (D.C.Cir. 1973), cert. denied, 415 U.S. 977 (1974),

      "In a large document it is vital that the agency specify in
      detail which portions of the document are disclosable and which
      are allegedly exempt."

484 F.2d at 827.  In addition, the agency must

      "provide particularized and specific justification for
      exempting information from disclosure."

Cuneo v. Schlesinger, 484 F.2d 1086,1092 (D.C.Cir. 1973), cert.
denied, 415 U.S. 977 (1974).  The FTC cannot deny disclosure, as it
has attempted to do here, merely by reliance on "general allegations
of exemption".  Ibid.

In Vaughn, the court required the agency to provide the requesting
party with a detailed index to the contents of the material whose
disclosure had been denied.  This requirement has become a commonly
accepted means of requiring the agency to meet its burden of

Federal Trade Commission
May 18, 1981
Page 4

substantiating a claim of privilege.  In Mead Data Control, Inc. v.
U.S. Dept. of the Air Force, 566 F.2d 242 (D.C.Cir. 1977), the court
specified the scope of this showing:

> "Thus, we require that when an agency seeks to withhold
> information it must provide a relatively detailed
> justification, specifically identifying the reasons why a
> particular exemption is relevant and correlating those claims
> with the particular part of a withheld document to which they
> apply."

566 F.2d at 251.  We expect this showing from the FTC.  If any
portions of the studies still considered to be exempt also contain
non-exempt material, we require that they be segregated in
accordance with the FOIA and the holding in Mead Data, supra, 566
F.2d at 260.

In particular, the courts have recognized that Exemption 5 does not
protect against the disclosure of purely factual material.  EPA v.
Mink, supra, at 89; Bristol-Myers Co. v. F.T.C., 424 F.2d 935
(D.C. Cir. 1970), cert. denied, 400 U.S. 824 (1970).  This holding,
originally developed in the context of the intra-agency memorandum
and executive privilege aspect of Exemption 5 has been found equally
applicable in the context of the work product privilege.  Robbins
Tire & Rubber Co. v. N.L.R.B., 563 F.2d 724,735 (5th Cir. 1977),
rev'd on other grounds, 437 U.S. 214 (1978); Deering Milliken, Inc.
v. Irving, 548 F.2d 1131,1138 (4th Cir. 1977); Sterling Drug, supra,
at 1027.  It is only mental impressions, not primary facts, which
the privilege protects.  Robbins Tire, supra.  We suspect that an
economic analysis of a national automobile industry must contain a
substantial amount of factual material which, unless inextricably
entwined with statements concerning litigation strategy in some as
yet unspecified proceeding, must be disclosed.

3.    The FTC Should Exercise Its Discretion to Disclose the
      Requested Information

As the notice of denial of our FOIA request correctly recognizes,
the release of data otherwise exempt from disclosure is within the
discretion of the FTC.  We believe this discretion should be
exercised in this case.  We do take issue, however, with the FTC's
demand for a statement as to our interest in the subject matter of
the data and the purpose to which we will put it, in order to
support our request for discretionary release.  It has been
repeatedly stated that

> "Under the FOIA...the interests and needs of the requesting
> party are irrelevant."

Federal Trade Commission
May 18, 1981
Page 5

Baker v. C.I.A., 580 F.2d 664,666 (D.C.Cir. 1978); EPA v. Mink, supra, at 92. If information is disclosable to one, it is disclosable to all. The interest "necessary" to invoke discretionary release is therefore not limited to that of the requester but may embrace the broader public interest. For purposes only of illustrating the public and private interests which compel discretionary disclosure, we offer the following.

We are general counsel to Automobile Importers of America, Inc., a trade association which includes virtually all United States importers, and foreign manufacturers, of automobiles. These companies are vitally interested in any governmental inquiry into automobile defects and the means by which these are to be remedied. Release of the studies would effectuate for these companies the primary purpose of the FOIA, which is to insure that government operates in the open. If the FTC is to take enforcement action on the basis of the material in these reports, our clients will want to know what that information was, and whether it supports and justifies the action taken. This knowledge is the only sure check on arbitrary agency action.

We therefore believe that even if the reports are exempt from disclosure by law, they should be released as a matter of agency discretion.

Respectfully submitted,

RIVKIN SHERMAN and LEVY

Dennis Adelson

Dennis A. Adelson

DAA:dlh

# APPENDIX D


IN THE UNITED STATES DISTRICT COURT
FOR THE DISTRICT OF COLUMBIA

NOVO LABORATORIES INCORPORATED
  59 Danbury Road
  Wilton, Connecticut 06879
  (203) 762-2401,

WALD, HARKRADER & ROSS
  1300 Nineteenth Street, N.W.
  Washington, D.C. 20036
  (202) 828-1200,

NORDISK-USA
  7315 Wisconsin Avenue
  Suite 851 W
  Bethesda, Maryland 20014
  (301) 656-5410,

PERITO, DUERK, CARLSON & PINCO, P.C.
  Suite 400
  1140 Connecticut Avenue, N.W.
  Washington, D.C. 20036
  (202) 659-8300,

                        Plaintiffs,

        v.                                Civil Action No. 80-1989

FEDERAL TRADE COMMISSION
  6th Street & Pennsylvania Ave., N.W.
  Washington, D.C. 20580,

MICHAEL PERTSCHUK
  Chairman of the Federal Trade
    Commission
  6th Street & Pennsylvania Ave., N.W.
  Washington, D.C. 20580,

PAUL RAND DIXON, DAVID A. CLANTON,
ROBERT PITOFSKY and PATRICIA P. BAILEY
  Members of the Federal Trade
    Commission
  6th Street & Pennsylvania Ave., N.W.
  Washington, D.C. 20580,

                        Defendants.

COMPLAINT FOR INJUNCTIVE RELIEF

Plaintiffs, for their complaint against Defendants herein, allege:

## JURISDICTION

1. This action is brought to compel Defendants to comply with the Freedom of Information Act, 5 U.S.C. § 552, and to obtain judicial review of agency action and inaction under the Administrative Procedure Act, 5 U.S.C. § 701 et seq. Plaintiffs seek an order (1) enjoining Defendants from unlawfully withholding documents responsive to Plaintiffs' Freedom of Information Act request, (2) requiring Defendants to produce all non-exempt documents for inspection and copying, (3) requiring Defendants to provide this Court and Plaintiffs with a detailed justification and index for all documents withheld, and (4) compelling Defendants to exercise their discretion to make exempt documents available to Plaintiffs.

2. This action arises under the Freedom of Information Act, 5 U.S.C. § 552, and the Administrative Procedure Act, 5 U.S.C. § 701 et seq. The jurisdiction of this Court is invoked pursuant to 5 U.S.C. § 552(a)(4)(B) and 28 U.S.C. §§ 1331 and 1361.

3. Venue is proper in this Court pursuant to 5 U.S.C. § 552(a)(4)(B), 5 U.S.C. § 703 and 28 U.S.C. § 1391.

4. There are no further administrative procedures available to Plaintiffs affording the relief sought herein.

## PARTIES

5. Plaintiff Novo Laboratories Incorporated ("Novo Labs") is a corporation organized and existing under the laws of the State of New York, with its offices and principal place of business in Wilton, Connecticut. Plaintiff is, inter alia, engaged in the distribution and sale in the United States of insulin for use in the treatment of diabetes.

6. Plaintiff Wald, Harkrader & Ross is a law firm with principal offices located in the District of Columbia. Wald, Harkrader & Ross represents Plaintiff Novo Laboratories before the Federal Trade Commission.

7. Plaintiff Nordisk-USA ("Nordisk") is a District of Columbia non-profit corporation qualified to do business as a foreign corporation in the State of Maryland, with its principal place of business located at Bethesda, Maryland. Plaintiff is, inter alia, engaged in the distribution and sale in the United States of insulin for use in the treatment of diabetes.

8. Plaintiff Perito, Duerk, Carlson & Pinco, P.C., is a law firm with offices located in the District of Columbia.  Perito, Duerk, Carlson & Pinco, P.C. represents Plaintiff Nordisk before the Federal Trade Commission.

9. Defendant Federal Trade Commission (hereinafter "Commission") is an agency of the United States and is subject to FOIA disclosure requirements.  Defendant has possession of the documents to which Plaintiffs seek access.

10. Defendant Michael Pertschuk is Chairman of the Federal Trade Commission and Defendants Paul Rand Dixon, David A. Clanton, Robert Pitofsky and Patricia P. Bailey are Members of the Federal Trade Commission.  As Commissioners of the agency in which the documents requested are located, Defendants are the custodians of those documents.  In addition, Defendants are responsible for the Commission's final denial of Freedom of Information Act requests.  They are sued herein in their official capacities.

## NATURE OF THE CONTROVERSY

11. By letter dated March 27, 1980 (Exhibit A), Plaintiff Perito, Duerk, Carlson & Pinco, P.C., by Frederick H. Graefe and acting on behalf of Plaintiff Nordisk, requested Defendant Federal Trade Commission to make available, under the Freedom of Information Act, documents concerning a specifically-identified agreement between Eli Lilly & Co. and Genentech Inc., including but not limited to the agreement itself.  The letter specifically requested that the Commission describe in detail any responsive material or documents withheld and specify the statutory basis for any such withholding.

12. By letter dated April 25, 1980 (Exhibit B), James A. Tobin, Acting Secretary of the Commission, acting on behalf of Defendants, granted Plaintiffs' request in part and denied it in part.  Defendants alleged generally that certain requested documents were exempt from public disclosure under 5 U.S.C. §§ 552(b)(4) and (5), but did not provide Plaintiffs with an index of documents withheld or attempt to relate the exemptions relied upon to specific documents.

13. By letter dated April 30, 1980 (Exhibit C), Plaintiff Wald, Harkrader & Ross, by Robert A. Skitol and acting on behalf of Plaintiff Novo Laboratories, joined in Plaintiffs Perito, Duerk, Carlson & Pinco, P.C.'s and Nordisk's initial request of March 27, 1980, by requesting copies of all documents released by the Commission in response to that initial request.

14. By letter dated May 20, 1980 (Exhibit D), Plaintiffs Perito, Duerk, Carlson & Pinco, P.C., by Frederick H. Graefe and acting on behalf of Plaintiff Nordisk, appealed the Acting Secretary's partial denial of the initial request of March 27,

1980.  The appeal letter specifically requested that if the Commission withheld any portion of the requested records, it provide with its final decision an index and itemization of the withheld records correlated to the alleged statutory justification for each withheld document.

15. By letters dated May 28, 1980 (Exhibits E and F), Plaintiff Wald, Harkrader & Ross, by Robert A. Skitol and acting on behalf of Plaintiff Novo Labortories, joined in Plaintiffs Perito, Duerk, Carlson & Pinco, P.C.'s and Nordisk's appeal and stated additional grounds for appeal of the initial denial of March 27, 1980.  In their appeal, Plaintiffs Wald, Harkrader & Ross and Novo Laboratories specifically requested that, even if responsive documents were, in the Commission's view, exempt from mandatory disclosure under the Freedom of Information Act, those documents be made available to Plaintiffs pursuant to the Commission's discretionary powers to do so.

16. By letter dated June 25, 1980 (Exhibit G), the Commission, through its Acting General Counsel, issued its final decision denying Plaintiffs' appeals.  In this letter, Defendants also specifically denied Plaintiffs' request for an index of the documents withheld and an identification of the basis for withholding each document.

17. Defendants' refusal to provide an index of the documents withheld and a justification for withholding such documents has made it impossible for Plaintiffs to determine the extent to which Defendants have complied with Plaintiffs' requests.  Plaintiffs, however, believe and allege that Defendants are unlawfully withholding some documents to which Plaintiffs are entitled.

### FIRST CAUSE OF ACTION

18.  Defendants' refusal to make available to Plaintiffs all or some of the records described as withheld in Defendants' responses to Plaintiffs' initial request of March 27, 1980 and to Plaintiffs' appeals of May 20, 1980 and May 28, 1980 is contrary to and in violation of the Freedom of Information Act, 5 U.S.C. § 552(a)(3).

19. Defendants' refusal to provide an index of documents withheld and a document-specific statement of the bases for withholding those documents is contrary to and in violation of the minimum standards of particularity and specificity imposed upon government agencies in responding to Freedom of Information Act requests.

### SECOND CAUSE OF ACTION

20. Plaintiffs hereby re-allege and incorporate herein by reference paragraphs 1-17 of this complaint.

21. On September 19, 1979, Defendants announced, and invited public comment upon, a proposed consent order against Eli Lilly and Co. ("Lilly") in settlement of charges that Lilly has unlawfully monopolized the U.S. finished insulin market.  Plaintiffs filed comments objecting to the proposed order on grounds, _inter alia_, that it provides inadequate relief with respect to new insulin technology which Lilly has acquired from Genentech, Inc.  That new technology was acquired by Lilly pursuant to the Lilly-Genentech agreement described in paragraph 11 hereinabove.

22. On June 17, 1980, Defendants accepted the proposed consent order and issued it in final form, notwithstanding Plaintiffs' objections.  One week later, by letter of June 25, 1980 (Exhibit G), Defendants issued their final decision denying Plaintiffs' request for access to the Lilly-Genentech agreement and related documents.

23. The withheld agreement and related documents bear directly upon the merits of Plaintiffs' objections to the aforementioned Lilly order.  Plaintiffs' ability fully and meaningfully to comment upon the order as proposed was impaired by Defendants' refusal to make said agreement and documents available to Plaintiffs during the comment period and/or prior to final action on said order.  Their ability now to assess the validity of Defendants' final action on that order is impaired by Defendants' final decision denying access to any such documents.

24. Defendants' refusal to exercise their discretion to make available to Plaintiffs all or some of the documents withheld notwithstanding their allegedly exempt status under the Freedom of Information Act, particularly in view of the central relevance of these documents to the issues surrounding the Lilly consent order, is arbitrary, capricious, an abuse of discretion and otherwise not in accordance with law, and constitutes agency action unlawfully withheld, within the meaning of the Administrative Procedure Act, 5 U.S.C. § 706.

PRAYER FOR RELIEF

WHEREFORE, Plaintiffs pray that:

(a) Defendants and their employees, agents and servants be enjoined from withholding the documents requested by Plaintiffs and be ordered to produce said documents promptly for Plaintiffs' inspection and copying;

(b) Defendants be required to provide Plaintiffs with a detailed and specific justification for withholding each such document and an itemized index that correlates statements in the justification with specific portions of each such document withheld;

(c) Pursuant to 5 U.S.C. § 552(a)(4)(D), this proceeding be given precedence on the docket over all cases, be assigned for hearing and trial and be expedited in every way;

(d) Pursuant to 5 U.S.C. § 552(a)(4)(E), Plaintiffs be awarded reasonable attorney fees and other costs incurred in this action; and

(e) This Court grant such other relfief as is just and proper in the premises.

Respectfully submitted,

Robert A. Skitol
Jeffrey F. Liss

WALD, HARKRADER & ROSS
1300 Nineteenth Street, N.W.
Washington, D.C. 20036
(202) 828-1200

Counsel for Plaintiffs Novo Labora-
    tories Incorporated and Wald,
    Harkrader & Ross

John P. Wintrol
Frederick H. Graefe

PERITO, DUERK, CARLSON & PINCO, P.C.
1140 Connecticut Ave., N.W., Suite 400
(202) 659-8300

Counsel for Plaintiffs Nordisk-USA
    and Perito, Duerk, Carlson & Pinco, P.C.

Dated: August 7, 1980